Fearless Investing Series: Mutual Funds Workbook ① ② ③

Diversify Your Fund Portfolio

Published by John Wiley & Sons, Inc., Hoboken, New Jersey.
Published simultaneously in Canada.

For general information about our other products and services, please contact our Customer Care Department within the United States at 800-762-2974, outside the United States at 317-572-3993 or fax 317-572-4002.

Wiley also publishes its books in a variety of electronic formats. Some content that appears in print may not be available in electronic books. For more information about Wiley products, visit our Web site at www.wiley.com.

ISBN 0-471-71186-1

Printed in the United States of America
10 9 8 7 6 5 4 3 2 1

Introduction

In the 1990s, it seemed that anyone could pick a strong-performing mutual fund and assemble a winning portfolio. With the tailwind of a buoyant market helping them, even relatively poor funds were able to score robust gains.

The past five years, however, have proved far more challenging for investors. Following a brutal bear market from 2000 through early 2003, the industry became engulfed in scandal, dogged by allegations of improper trading and unscrupulous sales practices.

Amid that backdrop, however, investors' faith in mutual funds as a fundamentally sound investment vehicle hasn't been shaken. Investors sent nearly $400 billion to mutual funds in 2003 and 2004. In so doing, they acknowledged that funds, with their built-in diversification and professional management, remain the best way for individuals to build long-term wealth.

We at Morningstar certainly believe that to be true. The year 2004 marked our company's 20th anniversary of providing investors with the information they need to make sound financial decisions. Along the way, we've talked to scores of investors who, empowered by Morningstar's objective research and analysis, have used mutual funds to achieve goals big and small: sending kids to college, remodeling houses, and enjoying worry-free retirements.

Helping even more investors reach their goals was the impetus behind Morningstar's new Fearless Investing Series. The series, as its name suggests, is designed to demystify the often-complex world of investing—and even make it fun. In addition to grounding you, the investor, in the basics of mutual funds, our interactive workbook series gives you concrete advice for selecting the best funds for you and putting the pieces together into a portfolio that delivers maximum long-term returns.

Although the books are sold individually, the three workbooks in the series are designed to be used in conjunction with one another. Book One, *Find the Right Mutual Funds*, provides an overview of how mutual funds work, as well as a discussion of how to evaluate a fund's manager, portfolio, risk/return potential, costs, and tax efficiency. Book Two, *Diversify Your Fund Portfolio*, discusses the keys to building a diversified, all-weather portfolio and gives you concrete pointers for selecting both bond and international funds. The series culminates with Book Three, *Maximize Your Fund Returns*. In this book, you'll find advanced strategies for maximizing your portfolio's return, along with our best tips for bear-proofing your portfolio and knowing when to sell.

Within each workbook, you'll find that we've divided each lesson into four distinct sections: the lesson itself, Fearless Facts, a quiz, and a worksheet. Each workbook also includes an Investing Terms section, a list of additional Morningstar resources, and a Recommended Reading section. Read on for details about how to get the most out of each section.

Lessons: The lessons are designed to give you an overview of a particular topic, along with plenty of real-life examples and concrete tips for putting the knowledge to work in your portfolio.

Fearless Facts: These scannable lists provide you with a quick overview of the key points from the lesson. Use our Fearless Facts to brush up on what you've just learned.

Quizzes: The quizzes help ensure that you've mastered the key concepts in the lesson. You'll find answers for each of the quizzes at the back of each book.

Worksheets: The worksheets are designed to help you put the key concepts in each lesson into practice. You'll find that many of the worksheets ask you to find facts about your own funds and portfolio; the goal of these exercises is to help you understand what you own and to ensure that your portfolio suits your goals and risk tolerance.

Investing Terms: Although Morningstar's Fearless Investing Series assumes that readers do not have any background in finance or investments and thus explains any term mentioned in the text, you can look to the Investing Terms section for a more in-depth definition of each term used in the series.

Additional Morningstar Resources: Morningstar's Fearless Investing Series is designed as an introduction to Morningstar's approach to selecting mutual funds and building portfolios. Investors interested in learning more about Morningstar's other products should consult this list.

Recommended Reading: This is a list of some of Morningstar's favorite books about mutual funds and investing.

Whether you're a novice investor or a seasoned hand looking to maximize your portfolio, we trust that you'll find Morningstar's Fearless Investing Series to be a practical and profitable way to learn about mutual funds and meet your financial goals. We wish you luck on your journey.

Acknowledgments

A number of individuals played a significant role in the production of the Fearless Investing Series. Susan Dziubinski, Peter Di Teresa, and David Harrell, developed most of the lessons that form the basis of the three books in the series. Scott Berry, Christopher Traulsen, Andrew Gogerty, Russel Kinnel, Kunal Kapoor, and Joseph Nasr also contributed valuable content. Morningstar's copy-editing staff, including Elizabeth Bushman and Jason Stipp, worked hard to ensure that the concepts in the book would be clear to novice investors.

Alla Spivak and Erica Moor shepherded the books through the publishing process, coordinating the work of all of the contributors. Morningstar's design staff, notably Lisa Lindsay, Minwha Kim, David Silva, and David Williams, developed the books' design. David Pugh, our editor at John Wiley & Sons, gave us valuable guidance for completing this book.

We also owe a huge debt of gratitude to Catherine Odelbo for helping develop the series' concept. As head of Morningstar's retail business unit, she has been central to putting Morningstar's motto of "Investors First" into action.

Finally, we're grateful to Morningstar founder Joe Mansueto, who founded this company on the principle that all investors are entitled to high-quality independent investment information. His company has grown by leaps and bounds since Joe founded it 20 years ago, but Morningstar has never deviated from that central principle.

Contents

Look Mutual Fund Risk in the Eye

Lesson 201: Benchmarks

The world's modern Hercules, Iranian Hossein Rezazadeh, hoisted more than 1,000 pounds in two lifts to claim the gold medal at the 2004 Athens Olympics. He may not have a perfect technique, but at a massive 352 pounds, Rezazadeh is a giant of a man who is unmatched in his weightlifting prowess.

The maximum weight that you can lift is often regarded as the definitive statement of your strength. Yet what actually constitutes a "good" bench-press depends on the person: A 5'5" man or woman who can bench-press 150 pounds may have a superior strength-to-bodyweight ratio compared with a 6'2" man or woman who can bench-press 250 pounds.

The same relativity holds true when examining a mutual fund's performance. What constitutes a "good" return depends on your needs and the type of fund. That's where benchmarks come in to play.

Your Personal Benchmark

Start by determining your personal benchmark. In fitness terms, that might mean getting strong enough to carry your 3-year-old around town without getting winded, or it might mean building up enough endurance to climb a mountain. In investment terms, it means setting a benchmark for the returns required to reach your investment goal, whether it is a long-term goal (retirement) or a short-term goal (buying a new house in two years).

Say you want to retire in 30 years. You may know how much money you have to invest today, you can anticipate how much you'll be able to invest in the future, and you have a rough idea how much you'll need in retirement. After crunching the numbers, let's say you find that you need an 8% return per year to meet your goal. That's your personal benchmark.

Identify your goals	Before you take out your checkbook, take some time to identify your goals. These goals are your personal benchmark, something to test the progress of your investment portfolio against.
	Ask yourself: 1. What do I want? 2. Is it attainable? 3. When do I need to reach this goal?

By knowing that benchmark, you can immediately rule out funds that rarely meet that hurdle each year, such as most bond funds. You can also rule out funds that can sometimes return much more than your personal benchmark because they probably present an added risk. That would include volatile fund types, such as emerging-markets funds or technology-sector funds. Why take on all that extra, unnecessary risk?

Indexes as Benchmarks

The most common type of performance benchmark is a market index—a preselected group of securities. Such indexes are usually tracked by the media and the investing community as indicators of the health of national and international stock and bond markets. Of course, there's no consensus on the single best index to use for investing purposes. The Dow Jones Industrial Average (DJIA) may be the index that heads the stock market report on the evening news, but it's rarely used as a performance benchmark for stock mutual funds. Why? Because it's so narrow: It includes just 30 large-company stocks, so it isn't all that indicative of the health of the overall stock market. The index you'll hear about most often in mutual fund circles is the Standard & Poor's 500 Index, which includes 500 major U.S. companies. The larger the company, the greater its position in the index. Because the stocks in the S&P 500 are chosen to cover a range of industry sectors, the index often paints a clearer picture of the overall market than the Dow Jones Industrial Average.

Home in on fund types with historical performances that match your goals. Saving for a retirement that won't begin for 30 years? You can afford a stock-heavy fund such as an S&P 500 index fund. Saving for college tuition that's due in 18 months? (They grow up fast!) You want to lock in your gains now and avoid losses, so a short-term bond fund may make sense.

Choose a benchmark

Yet despite its widespread appeal, the S&P 500's focus on large companies means it's not representative of the entire market and smaller stocks' performance in particular. It's therefore inappropriate to measure a fund that doesn't buy large companies, such as Third Avenue Value or T. Rowe Price Small-Cap Stock, against this benchmark only. Nor should you compare a foreign-stock fund like Vanguard International Growth with the S&P 500; that fund doesn't even own any U.S. stocks. And don't try to stack up bond funds against a stock-fund index like the S&P 500. This advice sounds like common sense, but investors make inappropriate comparisons all the time.

So what indexes can you use to make appropriate comparisons? The Russell 2000 Index, which tracks smaller U.S. companies, is a good tool to evaluate many small-company funds, while the Morgan Stanley Capital International Europe Australia Far East (MSCI EAFE) Index, which follows international stocks, is a good measuring stick for foreign funds. The Lehman Brothers Aggregate Bond Index is a good gauge for most taxable-bond funds. There are dozens of other indexes that segment the market even more, focusing on inexpensive large-company stocks or pricey small-company stocks, regions of the world such as Europe or the Pacific Rim, or even particular areas of the bond market. We include appropriate indexes for each fund on Morningstar.com.

Peer Groups as Benchmarks

The second type of benchmark you can use is peer groups, or funds that buy the same types of securities as your fund. Compare funds that buy large, undervalued companies with others with the same style—so-called large-value funds. Or compare those that buy only Latin American stocks with other funds that only buy Latin American stocks. That way, you're comparing apples to apples.

Morningstar categories are suitable peer-group benchmarks for most mutual funds. Depending on what a fund owns, it can land in one of more than 40 Morningstar categories. If a fund's portfolio features large-company stocks with high earnings growth, the fund is categorized as a large-growth fund. If the fund brims with smaller companies that are inexpensive, it lands in the small-cap value category. If U.S. government bonds that mature on average between one and four years populate the portfolio, the fund qualifies as a short-term government-bond fund.

What's so great about peer-group comparisons? They give you another way to examine a fund's performance. Consider Fidelity Blue Chip Growth. The fund's returns lagged the s&p 500 from 2001 through 2003. Against that benchmark, the fund looks like a dog. But against its peers, the fund looks pretty good this year: The average large-growth fund is down nearly 4% as of August 2004, but Fidelity Blue Chip Growth has lost just about 2%.

That might not be great performance for investors, but the fact that Fidelity Blue Chip Growth trails the s&p 500 this year isn't so much a reflection on the fund as it is on the relatively weak performance of large-growth stocks. After all, the s&p follows more than growth stocks; it has a hefty dose of value stocks, too. But large-growth stocks have been dawdling compared with more value-oriented fare in 2004. And since large-growth funds don't own such value-oriented stocks, the peer group is a better benchmark for Fidelity Blue Chip Growth than the s&p 500.

| Comparison shop | Once you have a goal in mind and a style that matches that goal, you're ready to comparison shop. Test any funds that catch your eye by checking to see how they stack up against like-minded rivals. |

Our Approach

When evaluating funds, select several benchmarks. Begin with your personal benchmark, and be sure that any investment you're considering can match your needs. Then compare the fund with a widely accepted index, such as the S&P 500, to get a sense of its performance on the broadest level. Finally, look to peer-group benchmarks to see if the fund is good at what it does.

Fearless Facts

▶ When it comes to mutual funds, the best-known index is probably the S&P 500, but there are thousands of offerings tracking hundreds of benchmarks. As long as you're clear about your goals, it's easy to find one that will suit you.

▶ Want to find out more about the actual index your fund copies? Morningstar tracks a lot of the benchmarks you might choose to emulate, including the S&P indexes and those from Russell, JP Morgan, and Lehman Brothers. We're confident that we cover most of the indexes you might seek. But if your fund is trying to mimic a very esoteric group of securities, you'll have to track down information about that index on your own.

▶ You can find references to public indexes anywhere, but you won't find the same peer groups anywhere but in Morningstar research. Generally, ratings and research agencies such as Morningstar create their own categories in order to better judge the funds they cover.

Quiz

1   Once you've calculated your personal benchmark, choose a fund that:

   a   Usually returns less than that benchmark.

   b   Usually returns more than that benchmark.

   c   Usually returns about the same as that benchmark.

Answers to this quiz can be found on page 233

2   Which is the best index to use when analyzing a U.S. large-company fund's performance?

   a   The Dow Jones Industrial Average.

   b   The S&P 500 Index.

   c   The MSCI EAFE Index.

3   Which is the best index with which to compare a small-company fund's performance?

   a   The S&P 500.

   b   The Russell 2000 Index.

   c   The Lehman Brothers Aggregate Bond Index.

4   Fund X underperformed the S&P 500 by five percentage points per year during the past five years, after beating the index by just as much in the three previous years. Fund X:

   a   Is a lousy fund.

   b   Probably owns something other than large-company stocks.

   c   Probably looks bad versus its Morningstar category, too.

continued...

5   What's the most appropriate benchmark to use when analyzing a
     large-cap growth fund?

a   The S&P 500.

b   Morningstar's large-cap growth category.

c . The Dow Jones Industrial Average.

Worksheet

What are your reasons for investing? What total return do you estimate your portfolio will need to earn for you to reach your goal?

Do the historical returns of the funds you own fit with the returns you're hoping to generate?

Take a look at the shareholder report for one or more of the mutual funds in your portfolio. What index does it use to benchmark its performance against? How has it fared against its benchmark over the past year? How about over the past three- and five-year periods? Has your fund consistently beaten its benchmark or underperformed it?

continued...

Next, go to your fund's Morningstar report on Morningstar.com. (Enter the ticker in the "Quotes/Reports" search box.) Check to see what Morningstar category your fund falls in, and compare your fund's performance with the category average. Does your fund outperform the group average on a regular basis? Why or why not?

Lesson 202: Looking at Historical Risk, Part One

Most natural risk-takers—mountain climbers, extreme athletes, motorcycle daredevils—tend to talk about the high of a job well done, an adventure completed, a successful free fall, and so on. They're less likely to dwell on comrades lost, bones broken, and the heavy insurance costs that surely dog them.

Investors tend to behave a little like these extreme athletes, at least when they're starting out: They would much rather talk about the returns their funds generated than the risks they took to achieve those returns or the losses they've incurred. Take Janus investors. Many of that shop's funds, including Janus Venture, enjoyed some heady years during the late 1990s. Venture shareholders were likely thrilled with their spectacular 141% return in 1999. But they probably weren't so thrilled when the fund lost 46% in 2000. Tremendous gains are won only through tremendous risk taking, which often means many ups and downs in short-term returns. That's called volatility.

While no single risk measure can predict with 100% accuracy how volatile a fund will be in the future, studies have shown that past risk is a pretty good indicator of future risk. In other words, if a fund has been volatile in the past, it's likely to be volatile in the future.

In this lesson, we'll tackle two common yardsticks for measuring a mutual fund's risk: standard deviation and beta. Both of these measures appear on a fund's Morningstar Fund Report.

Standard Deviation

Standard deviation is probably used more often than any other measure to gauge a fund's risk. Standard deviation simply quantifies how much a series of numbers, such as fund returns, varies around its mean, or average. Investors like using standard deviation because it provides a precise measure of how varied a fund's returns have been over a particular time frame—both on the upside and the downside. With this information, you can judge the range of returns your fund is likely to generate in the future. Morningstar calculates standard deviations for the most recent 36 months of a fund's life. The more a fund's returns fluctuate from month to month, the greater its standard deviation.

In brief	Standard deviation is just a statistical measure of how wide-ranging a fund's performance can be from year to year.

For instance, a mutual fund that gained 1% each and every month over the past 36 months would have a standard deviation of zero, because its monthly returns didn't change from one month to the next. But here's where it gets tricky: A mutual fund that lost 1% each and every month would also have a standard deviation of zero. Why? Because, again, its returns didn't vary. Meanwhile, a fund that gained 5% one month, 25% the next, and that lost 7% the next would have a much higher standard deviation; its returns have been more varied.

Standard deviation allows a fund's performance swings to be captured into a single number. For most funds, future monthly returns will fall within one standard deviation of its average return 68% of the time and within two standard deviations 95% of the time.

Let's translate. Say a fund has a standard deviation of four and an average return of 10% per year. Most of the time (or, more precisely, 68% of the time), we can expect the fund's future returns to range between 6% and 14%—or its 10% average plus or minus its standard deviation of four. Almost all of the time (95% of the time), its returns will fall between 2% and 18%, or within two standard deviations of its mean.

Over the Years Funds Have Generally Become More Volatile

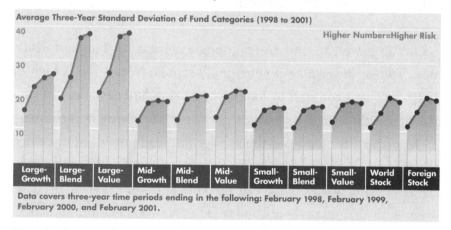

Average Three-Year Standard Deviation of Fund Categories (1998 to 2001)

Higher Number=Higher Risk

Large-Growth | Large-Blend | Large-Value | Mid-Growth | Mid-Blend | Mid-Value | Small-Growth | Small-Blend | Small-Value | World Stock | Foreign Stock

Data covers three-year time periods ending in the following: February 1998, February 1999, February 2000, and February 2001.

Most fund categories have experienced rising standard deviations, suggesting an increase in stocks' volatility overall—and hinting at potentially heightened risks for most investors' portfolios.

Using standard deviation as a measure of risk can have its drawbacks. It's possible to own a fund with a low standard deviation and still lose money. In reality, that's rare. Funds with modest standard deviations tend to lose less money over short time frames than those with high standard deviations. For example, the range of standard deviations among ultrashort-term bond funds, which are undoubtedly the lowest-risk funds around (other than money market funds), is a mere 0.1 to 1.3, with an average of 0.7%.

The bigger flaw with standard deviation is that it isn't intuitive. Sure, a standard deviation of seven is obviously higher than a standard deviation of five, but are those high or low figures? Because a fund's standard deviation is not a relative measure—which means it's not compared with other funds or with a benchmark—it is not very useful to you without some context.

So it's up to you to find an appropriate context for standard deviation. To help determine if your fund's standard deviation is high or low, we suggest you start by looking at the standard deviations of similar funds, those in the same category as the fund you're examining. In May 2002, for example, the average mid-cap growth fund carried a standard deviation of 36, while the typical large-value fund's standard deviation was 17.5. You can also compare a fund's standard deviation with that of a relevant index. The S&P 500, a common benchmark for large-cap funds, for example, had a standard deviation of 21.3 in mid-2002.

Three-Year Standard Deviation

U.S. Stock Funds				Taxable Bond Funds			
Investment Style				Duration			
Value	Blend	Growth		Short	Interm	Long	
			Market Cap				Quality
16.23	15.50	17.42	Large	2.69	4.96	11.08	High
17.03	17.96	19.47	Med	2.90	5.36	8.48	Med
19.60	20.52	22.80	Small	7.28	8.29	13.56	Low

Standard deviation, a measure of volatility, shows which investment styles have been the most (and least) risky over the past three years (through September 2004). The higher the number, the more volatile the funds in a given style box have been.

Beta

Beta, meanwhile, is a relative risk measurement because it depicts a fund's volatility against a benchmark. Morningstar calculates betas for stock funds using the s&p 500 Index as the benchmark. We also calculate betas using what we call a fund's best-fit index, which is the benchmark whose performance most resembles that of the fund. For bond funds, for example, we use the Lehman Brothers Aggregate Bond Index and best-fit indexes.

Beta is fairly easy to interpret. The higher a fund's beta, the more volatile it has been relative to its benchmark. A beta that is greater than 1.0 means that the fund is more volatile than the benchmark index. A beta of less than 1.0 means that the fund is less volatile than the index.

We're not making these up	Beta is a component of Modern Portfolio Theory (MPT), which is a standard method for assessing the performance of a fund. MPT has its roots in the academic study of stock and bond performance as it relates to the overall market.

In theory, if the market goes up 10%, a fund with a beta of 1.0 should go up 10%; if the market drops 10%, the fund should drop by an equal amount. A fund with a beta of 1.1 would be expected to gain 11% if the market rises by 10%, while a 10% drop in the market should result in an 11% drop by the fund. Conversely, a fund with a beta of 0.9 should return 9% when the market goes up 10%, but it should lose only 9% when the market drops 10%. The biggest drawback of beta is that it's really only useful when calculated against a relevant benchmark. If a fund is being compared with an inappropriate benchmark, its beta is meaningless.

There's another statistic that is often overlooked in this discussion of volatility: R-squared, which you can find on a fund's Fund Report. The lower the R-squared, the less reliable beta is as a measure of the fund's volatility. The closer to 100 the R-squared is, the more meaningful the beta is. Gold funds, for example, have an average R-squared of just three with the S&P 500, indicating that their betas relative to the S&P 500 are pretty useless as risk measures. Unless a fund's R-squared against the index is 75 or higher, disregard the beta.

Keep in mind:	A word about
▶ A higher R-squared often suggests a reliable beta figure. ▶ A lower R-squared often suggests that the beta will explain less of the fund's performance.	R-squared

Fearless Facts

▶ An annual gain of 50% isn't so exciting if your fund loses 98% the next year. Understanding a fund's volatility is a vital part of choosing the right fund for you.

▶ Standard deviation is the investment world's favorite measure of volatility. It expresses just how varied a fund's returns have been over some precise period of time. You can find the standard deviation of your fund on the fund company's Web site or on sites such as Morningstar.com.

▶ There are two major problems with standard deviation:

1. It doesn't identify poor performers. If a fund loses the same percentage of its assets year after year after year, there's no variance to its returns, right? So its standard deviation will be tremendously low and investors can get tricked into thinking it's a solid investment.

2. It doesn't identify good performers, either. It isn't a relative figure, so *you* have to do the extra research.

▶ When using standard deviation, you'll have to provide your own context. A diligent investor looks at standard deviation relative to that of other funds with a similar style.

▶ Don't forget beta! Beta provides some context for you, measuring the fund's volatility relative to its benchmark. If beta is greater than one, the fund is more volatile than the comparable index. If it's less than one, the fund is less jittery than the benchmark.

Quiz

1   What does standard deviation measure?

   a   When a fund's returns have beaten its peers' over a particular time period.

   b   How volatile a fund's returns have been versus a benchmark over a particular time period.

   c   How likely a fund is to lose money.

Answers to this quiz can be found on page 233

2   A fund has a standard deviation of 10 and an average return of 12% per year. What does that mean?

   a   Sixty-eight percent of the time, the fund's future returns will range between negative 8% and 32%.

   b   Ninety-five percent of the time, the fund's future returns will range between negative 8% and 32%.

   c   Ninety-five percent of the time, the fund's future returns will range between 2% and 22%.

3   To make the most of a fund's standard deviation, compare it with:

   a   The fund's R-squared.

   b   The fund's beta.

   c   The standard deviations of other funds in its category.

4   A fund with a beta of 1.20 will do what if the market falls 10%?

   a   Rise 20%.

   b   Fall 20%.

   c   Fall 12%.

continued...

5   You can draw the most accurate conclusions about the risks of
    which fund?

a	A fund with a beta of 1.10 and R-squared of 97.
b	A fund with a beta of 1.15 and an R-squared of 50.
c	A fund with a standard deviation of 20 and an R-squared of 95.

Worksheet

Look at the Morningstar report for one of your funds. What is the fund's standard deviation?

Compare the fund's standard deviation with that of other funds in the same category. Is its standard deviation high or low relative to its peers? Based on the standard deviation, would you expect your fund to fare well in a bear market, or poorly?

What is your fund's beta? Based on its beta, what can you tell about how volatile your fund is apt to be relative to its benchmark?

If your fund has a beta higher than its best-fit index, have its returns beaten the index? That is, has your fund given you extra returns to compensate for the extra risk it is taking on?

Look at your stock fund's R-squared value relative to the S&P 500. Based on what you see, would your fund be complementary with an S&P 500 Index fund, or redundant with it? Why?

Lesson 203: Looking at Historical Risk, Part Two

Until now, we've focused on risk measurements that you can find on most Web sites or in print publications. In this lesson, we'll discuss some only-from-Morningstar yardsticks you can use to get a handle on a fund's risk.

Why does Morningstar offer its own risk statistics when standard deviation and beta already exist as reliable statistics? Those figures give you an idea of how risky a fund is on an absolute level and as compared with an index. But as we pointed out in our last session, no single risk measurement can give you a full idea of a fund's volatility. If you approach risk from various angles—as Morningstar's measures do—you can get a much better picture of how a fund should behave. You can find all of these measures in a Morningstar Fund Report.

Morningstar Risk

Morningstar Risk score describes the variation in a fund's month-to-month returns. But unlike standard deviation, which treats upside and downside variability equally, the risk score places greater emphasis on downward variation, or losses.

The theoretical foundation for Morningstar Risk (and Morningstar's risk-adjusted return measure, also called the star rating) is relatively straightforward: The typical investor is risk-averse. Morningstar adjusts for risk by calculating a risk penalty for each fund based on that risk aversion. The risk penalty is the difference between a fund's raw return and its risk-adjusted return based on "expected utility theory," a commonly used method of economic analysis. Although the math is complex, the assumption is that investors prefer higher returns to lower returns, and—more importantly—prefer a more certain outcome to a less certain outcome. In other words, investors are willing to forego a small portion of a fund's expected return in exchange for greater certainty. Essentially, the theory rests on the assumption that investors are more concerned about a probable loss than an unexpectedly high gain.

At last! A measure you can really use	Morningstar's Risk score measurement doesn't compare your fund with some random index. Instead, it gives you a sense of how your fund stacks up relative to the competition. That's good news because two funds can post precisely the same annual returns, but Morningstar will spot the offering with the higher historical volatility and assign it a lower score.

Like beta, Morningstar's risk score is a relative measure. It compares the risk of funds in each Morningstar category. For example, a fund in the large-cap growth category is compared only with other funds in the same category. Likewise, a municipal-national short-term fund is compared only with offerings in the same category. This apples-to-apples comparison allows investors to evaluate the historical risk of funds that are likely to be considered for the same role in a broader portfolio.

Within each category, we rank each fund's risk penalty—the difference between its raw and risk-adjusted returns—from highest to lowest. A fund with greater variation in its month-to-month returns would be assessed a larger penalty than a fund with lesser variation. The level of risk is assigned based on the ranking for funds in the category: The top 10% of funds are High risk, the next 22.5% are Above Average risk, the middle 35% are Average risk, the next 22.5% are Below Average risk, and the bottom 10% are Low risk.

When using Morningstar Risk, remember that we set a fund's score based on its risk level relative to its category peers. You can't compare the Morningstar Risk score of funds from different categories, as you can their standard deviations. For example, an intermediate-term bond fund with High Morningstar Risk may be more volatile than other intermediate-term bond funds, but it could be—and, due to the nature of stock funds, probably is—less risky than a small-cap value fund with Below Average Morningstar Risk.

Bear-Market Rankings

Bear-market rankings compare how funds have held up during market downturns over the past five years. This measure is unlike the others presented thus far because it examines performance only during the times in which investors may face the largest potential for losses—during downturns, or corrections, in the market.

A bear market is officially defined as a sustained market correction, but for the purpose of these rankings, Morningstar identifies "bear-market months" that have occurred in the past five years. For stock funds, we consider any month in which the S&P 500 Index lost more than 3% to be a bear-market month. For bond funds, we count any month in which the Lehman Brothers Aggregate Bond Index lost more than 1%.

To generate our current bear-market rankings, we simply total each fund's performance during bear-market months over the past five years and separate them into 10 groups, from those with the most aggregate losses to those with the least. Funds with ranks of one or two withstood bear-market months better than those with ranks of nine or 10. If a stock fund receives a rank of 10, its performance during the bear-market months was among the worst 10% of all stock funds. A bear-market rank of one indicates that a fund ranked among the top 10% of all stock funds during those bear-market months. These scores can help predict which funds will hold up well should the market undergo another correction.

Bear-market rankings have two major drawbacks. First, these measures let you know how a fund performed only during certain time periods. Although it's helpful to know how your fund performed during these market downturns, the fund could certainly lose money—lots of it—during a market upturn, too. Gold funds, for instance, often earn decent bear-market ranks, but they lose money at other times and are not considered low-risk investments.

The second drawback to bear-market rankings is that not all bear markets are the same. The next market correction may be caused by different economic forces than those that led to the previous one. Hence, funds that held up well in one bear market may not do so well in the next. Conversely, funds that were pummeled the last time around might shine in the next bear market.

All of the risk measurements we've discussed are based solely on past performance. By definition, they fail to account for any future risks a fund might harbor. For example, a fund that used to own mostly low-key large-company stocks may now be heavily invested in smaller companies, and therefore it may be taking on more risk than its historical measures show. Given this limitation, remember that statistical risk measures are a good way to begin understanding a fund's risk, but they're not guarantees of safety.

Fearless Facts

▶ Relativity matters. One relative risk measure is the Morningstar Risk score. This score is something like beta in that it compares your fund with other investment offerings. But the Morningstar Risk score gives you more relevant information.

▶ The Morningstar Risk score focuses on losses. No one is too worried if their fund posts outsized gains, right? So Morningstar punishes losses more than it penalizes gains in producing its score.

▶ The Morningstar Risk score compares your funds with other funds in its Morningstar category, rather than with some random index or benchmark.

▶ There are more ways than one to assess relative risk. You should know how your fund performs when markets turn sour. Check the fund's bear-market rankings. Bear-market rankings grade funds based on their performance in tough markets (defined as months in which the S&P 500 loses more than 3% or, for bond funds, months in which the Lehman Brothers Aggregate Index loses more than 1%).

Quiz

1   Morningstar Risk measures how volatile a fund is:

a	Relative to an index.
b	Relative to others in its category.
c	During market corrections.

Answers to this quiz can be found on page 234

2   If you want to compare how volatile a bond fund and a stock fund are, use:

a	Morningstar Risk.
b	Morningstar's bear-market rankings.
c	Standard deviation.

3   What's the best way to use bear-market rankings?

a	To find funds that don't exhibit wild performance swings.
b	To find funds that tend to do relatively well when the market falls.
c	To find funds that will definitely do well in the next bear market.

4   Morningstar Risk is based on the idea that investors are more concerned about:

a	Unexpectedly high gains.
b	The chance of losing money.
c	Maximizing uncertainty.

5   Morningstar Risk describes the variation in a fund's:

a	Annual returns.
b	Daily returns.
c	Monthly returns.

Worksheet

Look at the Morningstar report for one of your funds. What is your fund's overall Morningstar Risk score? What does this tell you about how your fund has performed when the market has been down? How does its Morningstar Risk score compare with that of other funds in the same category?

What is your fund's bear-market ranking? Does this figure tell you anything about how that fund might perform in the next bear market?

Can you use risk measurements to forecast future risks and returns?

Lesson 204: Gauging Risk and Return Together, Part One

Up until now, we've focused on yardsticks that tell you either how good or how volatile a fund's returns have been. But there are also measures that treat performance and risk together: risk-adjusted performance measures. We'll cover two of the more common yardsticks, alpha and the Sharpe ratio, in this lesson. You can find both of these figures on the Morningstar Fund Report.

Alpha Defined

In a nutshell, alpha is the difference between a fund's expected returns based on its beta and its actual returns. Alpha is sometimes interpreted as the value that a portfolio manager adds, above and beyond a relevant index's risk/reward profile. If a fund returns more than what you'd expect given its beta, it has a positive alpha. If a fund returns less than its beta predicts, it has a negative alpha.

Sometimes fund shops that use a lot of jargon will cite their fund's alpha figures as proof that they've pulled in star talent. That doesn't make a lot of sense until you see alpha as a way to express the difference between how the fund should have performed, given its risk profile, and how it did perform. As long as that number is positive, fund shops like to claim that that difference is due to management technique. Of course, when the number is negative, fund shops scramble to make excuses.

Alpha managers

As you'll recall from our earlier lesson on risk, beta tells you how much you can expect a fund's returns to move up or down given a gain or loss of its benchmark. For example, if the ABC Fund has a beta of 1.1 in comparison with the S&P 500 and the S&P 500 returns 30% for the year, you would expect ABC Fund to return 33%. (30% x 1.1 = 33%.) Since mutual funds don't necessarily produce the returns predicted by their betas, alpha can be helpful to investors.

To calculate a fund's alpha, first subtract the return of the 90-day Treasury bill, for whatever time period you want to measure, from the fund's raw return. What does a government bond have to do with all this? The T-bill serves as a proxy for a risk-free investment, and we're assuming that the return of a mutual fund should, at the very least, exceed that of a risk-free investment. This figure gives you the fund's excess return over the risk-free, guaranteed investment. From that, subtract the fund's expected excess return based on its beta. What's left over is the alpha.

What is Alpha?

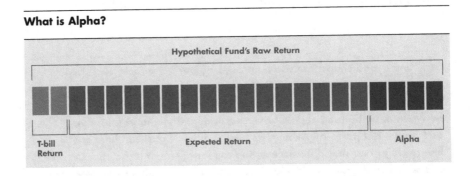

Hypothetical Fund's Raw Return

T-bill Return   Expected Return   Alpha

Because a fund's return and its risk both contribute to its alpha, two funds with the same returns could have different alphas. Further, if a fund has a high beta, it's quite possible for it to have a negative alpha. That's because the higher a fund's risk level (beta), the greater the returns it must generate in order to produce a high alpha. Just as a teacher would expect his or her students in an advanced class to work at a higher level than those in a less-advanced class, investors expect more return from their higher-risk investments.

How to Use Alpha

It seems to follow, then, that you would want to find high-alpha funds. After all, these are funds that are delivering returns higher than they should be, given the amount of risk they assume.

But alpha has its quirks. First, it's dependent on the legitimacy of the fund's beta measurement. After all, it measures performance relative to beta. So, for example, if a fund's beta isn't meaningful because its R-squared is too low (below 75), its alpha isn't valid, either.

Second, alpha fails to distinguish between underperformance caused by incompetence and underperformance caused by fees. For example, because managers of index funds don't select stocks, they don't add or subtract much value. Thus, in theory, index funds should carry alphas of zero. Yet many index funds have negative alphas. Here, alpha usually reflects the drag of the fund's expenses.

Finally, it's impossible to judge whether alpha reflects managerial skill or just plain old luck. Is that high-alpha manager a genius, or did he just stumble upon a few hot stocks? If it's the latter, a positive alpha today may turn into a negative alpha tomorrow.

The Sharpe Ratio Defined

The Sharpe ratio uses standard deviation to measure a fund's risk-adjusted returns. The higher a fund's Sharpe ratio, the better a fund's returns have been relative to the risk it has taken on. Because it uses standard deviation, the Sharpe ratio can be used to compare risk-adjusted returns across all fund categories.

And the star is...	The Sharpe ratio is often considered an accurate indicator of a fund's risk/reward profile because it takes into account so many other measures. That makes for a pretty complete package.

Developed by its namesake, Nobel Laureate William Sharpe, this measure quantifies a fund's return in excess of our proxy for a risk-free, guaranteed investment (the 90-day Treasury bill) relative to its standard deviation. To calculate a fund's Sharpe ratio, first subtract the return of the 90-day Treasury bill from the fund's returns, then divide that figure by the fund's standard deviation. If a fund produced a return of 25% with a standard deviation of 10 and the T-bill returned 5%, the fund's Sharpe ratio would be 2.0: $(25-5) \div 10$.

The higher a fund's Sharpe ratio, the better its returns have been relative to the amount of investment risk it has taken. For example, both State Street Global Research and Morgan Stanley Inst. European Real Estate have enjoyed heady three-year returns of 23.9% through August 2004. But Morgan Stanley sports a Sharpe ratio of 1.09 versus State Street's 0.74, indicating that Morgan Stanley took on less risk to achieve the same return.

The higher a fund's standard deviation, the larger the denominator of the Sharpe ratio equation; therefore, the fund needs to generate high returns to earn a high Sharpe ratio. Conversely, funds with modest standard deviations can carry high Sharpe ratios if they generate good returns.

How to Use the Sharpe Ratio

The Sharpe ratio has a real advantage over alpha. Remember that standard deviation measures the volatility of a fund's return in absolute terms, not relative to an index. So whereas a fund's R-squared must be high for alpha to be meaningful, Sharpe ratios are meaningful all the time.

Moreover, it's easier to compare funds of all types using the standard-deviation-based Sharpe ratio than with beta-based alpha. Unlike beta—which is usually calculated using different benchmarks for stock and bond funds—standard deviation is calculated the exact same way for any type of fund, be it stock or bond. We can therefore use the Sharpe ratio to compare the risk-adjusted returns of stock funds with those of bond funds.

As with alpha, the main drawback of the Sharpe ratio is that it is expressed as a raw number. Of course, the higher the Sharpe ratio the better. But given no other information, you can't tell whether a Sharpe ratio of 1.5 is good or bad. Only when you compare one fund's Sharpe ratio with that of another fund (or group of funds) do you get a feel for its risk-adjusted return relative to other funds.

Fearless Facts

▶ Familiarize yourself with tools that will allow you to assess performance and volatility.

▶ Know your alpha. This figure, which is available from the mutual fund company and on the fund's Morningstar report, allows you to assess risk and return.

▶ Alpha is calculated by measuring the difference between what you actually got from the fund (its returns) and what you expected from the fund (based on its beta). If this measurement is positive, the fund does better than you might predict given its beta. If the measurement is negative, the fund does a bit worse than you might expect (again, given its beta). Are you catching on to a trend here? It's all relative.

▶ The Sharpe ratio brings it all together. Like alpha, this figure is available from fund shareholder reports or in the fund's Morningstar report.

▶ Remember, the Sharpe ratio is one of the most reliable measurements of risk and return available to investors. It measures the difference between a fund's return and a risk-free investment (usually a 90-day Treasury bill). It divides that difference by the fund's standard deviation and comes up with a score—the Sharpe ratio.

▶ A pretty good rule of thumb is to stick with funds that sport fairly high Sharpe ratios. This figure suggests that the fund's returns have been strong relative to its risk profile.

49

Quiz

1 A fund with a negative alpha:

    a Has returned more than you'd expect, given its beta.

    b Has returned less than you'd expect, given its beta.

    c Has returned less than you'd expect, given its standard deviation.

Answers to this quiz can be found on page 235

2 Funds A, B, and C each return 15%, while the S&P 500 returns 10%. Relative to the S&P 500, which fund has the highest alpha?

    a Fund A, which has a beta of 1.0.

    b Fund B, which has a beta of 1.7.

    c Fund C, which has a beta of 0.8.

3 Which measurement is most useful to investors?

    a An alpha of 1.3 for a fund with a beta of 1.1 and an R-squared of 50.

    b An alpha of -0.5 for a fund with a beta of 0.9 and an R-squared of 70.

    c A Sharpe ratio of 1.7 for a fund with a standard deviation of 12%.

4 If a fund returned 30% with a standard deviation of 15%, and the 90-day Treasury bill returned 3%, what's the fund's Sharpe ratio?

    a 1.8.

    b 2.0.

    c 2.2.

5 The higher a fund's Sharpe ratio:

    a The greater its risk.

    b The greater its returns.

    c The greater its returns given the amount of risk it's taking on.

Worksheet

Look at a Morningstar report for one of the funds in your portfolio. What is your fund's alpha? What does this tell you about your fund's performance? Its risk?

What is your fund's Sharpe ratio? How does your fund's standard deviation factor into its Sharpe ratio?

What do you think is the best way to use the Sharpe ratio to evaluate a fund's risk/reward profile? Should you just go with the fund with a highest Sharpe ratio? Should you compare your fund's Sharpe ratio with the category average?

Which measure do you think is the best to use to evaluate a fund's risk/reward profile? The Morningstar risk-adjusted rating (the star rating)? Alpha? The Sharpe ratio? Why?

Lesson 205: Gauging Risk and Return Together, Part Two

Our last lesson focused on two common measures of risk-adjusted performance: alpha and the Sharpe ratio. But as we pointed out, both of those figures need a context to be useful. Who can say whether an alpha of 0.7 is good? Or whether a Sharpe ratio of 1.3 is good?

That's where Morningstar's proprietary fund rating, often called the star rating, comes in. Unlike alpha and the Sharpe ratio, the Morningstar Rating for Funds puts data into context, making it more intuitive. You can find a fund's Morningstar Rating on its Morningstar Fund Report.

What is the Star Rating?

Let's clear the air immediately: The star rating is a purely mathematical measure that shows how well a fund's past returns have compensated shareholders for the amount of risk it has taken on. Morningstar fund analysts don't assign star ratings and have no subjective input into the ratings. Morningstar doesn't subtract stars from funds we don't like or add stars when we do.

The Morningstar Rating is a measure of a fund's risk-adjusted return, relative to similar funds. Funds are rated from 1 to 5 stars, with the best performers receiving 5 stars and the worst performers receiving a single star.

Morningstar gauges a fund's risk by calculating a risk penalty for each fund based on "expected utility theory," a commonly used method of economic analysis. It assumes that investors are more concerned about a possible poor outcome than an unexpectedly good outcome, and those investors are willing to give up a small portion of an investment's expected return in exchange for greater certainty.

What the star rating doesn't do	The star rating is a quick way to get a sense of a fund's risk/reward profile relative to its rivals in its Morningstar category. It's worth pointing out, though, that that means that every fund is running in a pretty big pack, with index funds competing against growth-oriented large-blend funds and so on. It's just one more reason to see the star rating as a starting point for your decision-making process.

Consider a simple example—a fund expected to return 10% each year. Investors are likely to receive 10%, but past variations in the fund's return suggest there's a chance they might end up with anywhere from 5% to 15%. While receiving more than 10% would be a pleasant surprise, most investors are likely to worry more about receiving less than 10%. Hence, they'd probably be willing to settle for a slightly lower return—say 9%—if they could be reasonably certain they'd receive that amount. If a fund expected to return 10% each year, but variations in its past returns suggested a narrower 8% to 12% range, investors wouldn't want to forego as much of the expected return in exchange for increased certainty.

This concept is the basis for how Morningstar adjusts for risk. A "risk penalty" is subtracted from each fund's total return, based on the variation in its month-to-month return during the rating period, with an emphasis on downward variation. The greater the variation, the larger the penalty. If two funds have the exact same return, the one with more variation in its return is given the larger risk penalty. Funds are ranked within their categories according to their risk-adjusted returns (after accounting for all sales charges and expenses). The 10% of funds in each category with the highest risk-adjusted return receive 5 stars, the next 22.5% receive 4 stars, the middle 35% receive 3 stars, the next 22.5% receive 2 stars, and the bottom 10% receive 1 star.

How Does It Work?

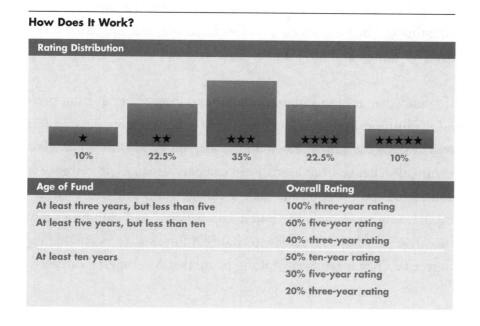

Rating Distribution

★	★★	★★★	★★★★	★★★★★
10%	22.5%	35%	22.5%	10%

Age of Fund	Overall Rating
At least three years, but less than five	100% three-year rating
At least five years, but less than ten	60% five-year rating
	40% three-year rating
At least ten years	50% ten-year rating
	30% five-year rating
	20% three-year rating

For multi-share–class funds, each share class is rated separately and counted as a fraction of a fund within this scale, which may cause slight variations in the distribution percentages. This accounting prevents a single portfolio with multiple share classes in a smaller category from dominating any portion of the rating scale.

Funds are rated for up to three periods—the trailing three, five, and ten years—and ratings are recalculated each month. Funds with less than three years of performance history are not rated. For funds with only three years of performance history, their three-year star ratings will be the same as their overall star ratings. For funds with five-year records, their five-year histories will count for 60% of their overall rating and their three-year rating will count for 40% of the overall rating. For funds with more than a decade of performance, the overall rating will be weighted as 50% for the ten-year rating, 30% for the five-year rating, and 20% for the three-year rating.

If a fund changes Morningstar categories during the evaluation period, its historical performance within the other category is given less weight in its star rating, based on the magnitude of the change. (For example, a change from a small-cap category to large-cap category is considered more significant than a change from mid-cap to large-cap.) Doing so ensures the fairest comparisons and minimizes any incentive for fund companies to change a fund's style in an attempt to receive a better rating by shifting to another Morningstar category.

Caveats

Like all backward-looking measures, the star rating has limitations. It is critical to remember that the rating is not a forward-looking, forecasting tool. The rating won't predict short-term winners. The star rating is best used as an initial screen to identify funds worthy of further research—those that have performed well on a risk-adjusted basis relative to their peers.

> The big difference between Morningstar's star ratings and the Sharpe ratio, alpha, and the Modern Portfolio Theory is that Morningstar puts its rating into context. It rates funds relative to other offerings in their categories, rather than comparing the fund with an outside benchmark.

Bringing it into focus

The star rating is a strictly quantitative measure—a high rating doesn't imply the approval or endorsement of a fund by a Morningstar analyst. Additionally, if a management change occurs, the ratings stay with the fund, not with the portfolio manager. Therefore, a fund's rating might be based almost entirely on the success of a manager who is no longer with the fund.

Also, because funds are rated within their respective categories, it's important to note that not all 5-star funds are equal or even interchangeable. A 5-star sector fund, for example, might have the best risk-adjusted return within its specific category, but it's probably far riskier than a highly rated diversified fund.

Rather than buying funds based on their ratings, investors should first decide on an overall portfolio strategy and then seek the best funds for each portion of their portfolios. Use the star rating as a first screen.

Fearless Facts

▶ The Morningstar Star Rating is a measure of the fund's risk-adjusted return relative to other funds in its category over the past 3, 5, and 10 years.

▶ Know your fund's star rating, but don't believe the hype. Understand that just because your fund received a 5-star rating doesn't mean that you received a windfall. It just means that your fund did better on a risk/reward basis than 90% of its competitors in the category. (Of course, the whole gang could have taken a nose-dive, as Asian equity funds did in 1998.)

▶ Know the limitations of the star rating. Understand that the star rating isn't ever-sustainable: The rating is a backward-looking score, and past performance is no indication of future results. Changes may affect the legitimacy of your star rating too: Has your fund shifted categories recently? Does the offering have a new manager?

Quiz

1 Star ratings are:

a Assigned by analysts.

b Short-term predictive measures.

c Mathematical measures of risk-adjusted performance.

Answers to this quiz can be found on page 235

2 Which statement is false?

a Star ratings measure a fund's risk-adjusted performance against funds in the same category.

b A fund must have at least three years of performance history to qualify for a star rating.

c A fund automatically loses a star if its manager leaves.

3 Which fund probably earns a 5-star rating?

a A fund with extraordinary returns and low risk.

b A fund with very low returns and average risk.

c A fund with average returns and average risk.

4 The Morningstar Rating is meant to identify funds that:

a Will have the best short-term returns in the future.

b Every investor should own.

c Could be worthy of future research.

5 Morningstar will only rate a fund if:

a It has at least three years of performance history.

b It has at least ten years of performance history.

c The fund manager is nice to us.

Worksheet

Look at a Morningstar report for one the funds in your portfolio. What is its Morningstar star rating? What does this rating measure? If your fund has a high star rating, is the manager responsible for that high star rating still working on the fund?

Pick out any two 5-star funds from different categories. Compare their returns, betas, standard deviations, and Sharpe ratios. How are they different? Even though they are both 5-star funds, do you think one would be a better investment than the other? Why or why not?

Should you base investment decisions on the Morningstar star rating or any other risk/reward statistic? If not, how should you use these statistics to make investment decisions?

Lesson 206: Examining a Stock Fund's Portfolio, Part One

Most of us wouldn't buy a new home just because it looked good from the outside. We would do a thorough walk-through first. We'd examine the furnace. We'd check for a leaky roof. We'd look for cracks in the foundation.

Mutual fund investing requires the same careful investigation. You need to do more than give a fund a surface-level once-over before investing in it. Knowing that the fund has been a good risk-adjusted performer for investors in the past isn't enough to merit a financial commitment from you today. You need to understand what's inside the fund's portfolio now—or how it invests.

Such information, which tells you how your fund will likely behave, helps you set realistic expectations for your investment. A fund manager who quickly buys and sells a compact portfolio of high-priced, fast-growing companies will produce different results from a manager who owns 300 stocks of larger companies with lower earnings but cheap prices. Further, unless you know what a fund owns, you can't determine what role the fund fills in your portfolio. For a fund to fill the large-cap growth portion of your portfolio, you need to know that it actually invests in large-growth companies. Finally, examining a fund's portfolio can tip you off to risks the fund may be harboring—risks that might not have surfaced yet.

For U.S. stock funds, you'll want to know a handful of things, starting with the size of the companies in which the fund invests, as well as how much the manager is willing to pay for these companies and how quickly they're growing. A quick way to identify the relative size and characteristics of the stocks a fund owns is the Morningstar style box, which appears on the Morningstar Fund Report.

The Style Box Defined

The Morningstar style box is a nine-square grid that gives you a quick and clear picture of a fund's investment style. The style box classifies funds by whether they own large-, mid-, or small-capitalization stocks, and by whether those stocks have growth or value characteristics or land somewhere in between.

Using the Morningstar Style Box

Level of Risk	Investment Style			Median Market Cap
	Value	Blend	Growth	
○ Low	Large-Cap Value	Large-Cap Blend	Large-Cap Growth	Large
◐ Moderate	Mid-Cap Value	Mid-Cap Blend	Mid-Cap Growth	Medium
● High	Small-Cap Value	Small-Cap Blend	Small-Cap Growth	Small

The Morningstar style box is a nine-square grid that provides a quick and clear picture of a fund's investment style.

We'll look first at the stock size and growth and value dimensions and then explore the ways in which they come together in the style box.

Company Size. Every month, Morningstar classifies all stocks in its database according to their market capitalizations, or the total market value of all outstanding stock shares. Take supermarket chain Winn-Dixie Stores. Back in 2002, its 143.1 million shares went for $18.17 each (May 20, 2002), giving the company a market capitalization of $2.6 billion (143.1 million × $18.17).

Of course, we also want to know how Winn-Dixie's size stacked up against other companies. Did a market capitalization of $2.6 billion mean that Winn-Dixie was big? Small? In between?

Morningstar ranks all U.S. stocks by their market capitalizations each month, classifying the companies that make up the top 72% of the domestic U.S. market as large-capitalization (large-cap) stocks, the next 18% as mid-cap, and the smallest 10% as small-cap stocks. As of April 2002, stocks with market caps of more than $8.85 billion were considered large caps; companies with market caps between $1.56 billion and $8.85 billion were considered mid-caps; and those with less than $1.56 billion were classified as small caps. That made Winn-Dixie a mid-cap stock.

How things change. The past two years haven't been kind to this company, which suffered relative to its large competitors, many of whom acquired smaller stores and merged with other strong rivals. The stock's share price has dropped to $5.55, its median market capitalization now hovers at about $789 million, and if you're looking to locate it in Morningstar's style box, you'll have to find the small-value square.

Growth and Value Metrics. Morningstar determines a fund's style— whether it invests in "growth" or "value" stocks—by applying a set of five growth metrics and a set of five value metrics to each individual stock the fund holds. These characteristics are compared with those of other stocks within the same capitalization band, arriving at a score for each company that ranges from zero to 100. For the purpose of Morningstar's style box, we group each stock into one of seven style "zones" based on geographic locales: the United States, Latin America, Canada, Europe, Japan, Asia (excluding Japan), and Australia/ New Zealand.

When it comes to size, there are no rules	By now you know that Morningstar is a big fan of relative measurements. Thus, we don't adopt unchanging cut-off points for style box measurements. That means that even if your fund manager is a buy-and-hold investor, your fund could bounce around the style box a bit.

We begin by measuring the "value" aspects of a stock by comparing the price of one share of a stock with the company's projected earnings per share. In its heyday, Winn-Dixie's $18.50 stock price was divided by its projected earnings per share for the following year ($1.08) for a forward price/earnings ratio (P/E) of 18. In other words, investors were paying $18 for every $1 in earnings that Winn-Dixie generated. This metric was ranked against other stocks within the United States style zone, and the result made up 50% of Winn-Dixie's value score.

The other 50% of the value score comes from four equally weighted historical measures: a stock's price/sales (P/S), price/book (P/B), and price/cash flow (P/CF) ratios, as well as its dividend yield. We rank these measures against those of other U.S. stocks in the mid-cap range and their combined rankings go into Winn-Dixie's value score.

The growth score similarly uses one forward-looking measure and four equally weighted historical metrics. Half of the stock's growth score comes from ranking its long-term projected earnings growth rate against those of other U.S. stocks in the same capitalization band. Winn-Dixie's 6.75% projected growth rate ranked above average (it was in the 65th percentile). Next, we ranked Winn-Dixie based on its historical earnings growth, sales, cash flow, and book-value growth rates against other U.S. stocks in its market-cap band. The resulting rankings made up the other 50% of Winn-Dixie's growth score.

We calculate a stock's style score by subtracting its value score from its growth score, resulting in scores that can range from -100 to 100. A stock with a style score of -100 would be a cheap, high-yielding, low-growth stock, while one with a score of 100 would have no yield and very high historical and projected growth rates. We classify stocks in the middle as "core" stocks. The dividing lines between value, core, and growth can vary over time with changes in the market, but on average each style will include approximately one-third of all stocks in each market-cap range.

Tackling the Funds. Once we have analyzed the stocks, figuring out where a fund's portfolio lands in the style box is easy. First, we calculate the geometric mean of the market capitalizations of all of the stocks a fund owns. This means that we don't just calculate a straight average of a fund's stocks' market caps. Instead, the calculation takes into account the market cap of each stock and the portion of the portfolio that it makes up to come up with a number that best represents how the portfolio as a whole is positioned.

We then compare that market-cap average with the stocks in its geographic style zone. If a fund's market-cap average is at least as big as the top 70% of the capitalization of its style zone, it is classified as a large-cap fund. If the market-cap average falls in the next-largest 20% of its style zone, it is a mid-cap fund. We classify any fund with a market cap below that as small cap.

Value and growth at the stock level	Morningstar analysts determine the investment style of individual firms, using scores drawn from both forward-looking and historical measures of the firm.		
	Kinds of Measures	**Value Score**	**Growth Score**
	Forward-Looking Measures	Price/Projected Earnings	Long-term Projected Earnings Growth
	Historical-Based Measures	Dividend Yield	Historical Earnings Growth
		Price/Book	Sales Growth
		Price/Sales	Cash-Flow Growth
		Price/Cash Flow	Book-Value Growth

To determine the overall style score for a fund, we take the style score for each stock in the portfolio and determine the average weighted score for the portfolio in aggregate. The resulting number can range from 100 (for a fund with nothing but low-yield, extremely growth-oriented stocks) to −100 (a fund emphasizing cheap, high-yield, low-growth stocks). A portfolio is classified as growth if the net score equals or exceeds the "growth threshold" (normally about 25 for large-cap stocks). It is deemed value if its score equals or falls below the "value threshold" (normally about −15 for large-cap stocks). And if the score lies between the two thresholds, the portfolio is classified as "blend." (Morningstar classifies individual stocks landing between value and growth as "core.")

Just as with individual stocks, the thresholds between value, blend, and growth funds vary to some degree over time, as the distribution of stock styles changes in the market. However, on average, the three fund styles each account for approximately one-third of each market-cap range.

Putting the Morningstar Style Box to Work

When you look at a fund's Morningstar style box, you immediately get some insight into the manager's investment strategy. A growth portfolio will mostly contain higher-priced companies that the manager believes have the potential to increase earnings faster than the rest of the market. A value orientation, on the other hand, means the manager buys stocks that are cheap, but that could eventually see their worth recognized by the market. A blend fund will mix the two philosophies: The portfolio may contain growth stocks and value stocks, or it may contain stocks that exhibit both characteristics.

Because the style box shows you how a fund actually invests, you can use it to get an idea of what sort of risks the fund harbors today. A fund that owns smaller, more expensive stocks is bound to be more volatile than one holding large, cheap names. And the style box allows you to quickly see where a fund's portfolio lands.

Fearless Facts

▶ Always read the ingredients. It's important to know what your fund owns. The best investors are often those who can recite a few of their fund's top holdings and can understand why the fund owns them.

▶ Morningstar's style box helps you understand the nature of your portfolio; it reflects the size—large, medium, or small—and style—growth, blend, or value—of the companies that your fund owns.

▶ Know the limitations of the style box: Morningstar calculates an overall style score for each fund, using the average weighted score for the portfolio in aggregate. This score is just an average; that means that your fund might end up in the small-value square of the box even though it holds one or two large-blend names.

▶ Use the style box as the first step in understanding your portfolio, but get ready to dig deeper.

Quiz

1   The Morningstar style box does not summarize which of the following?

   a   The size of the stocks the fund owns.

   b   The value or price of the stocks the fund owns.

   c   How rapidly a fund manager buys and sells stocks.

Answers to this quiz can be found on page 236

2   What is a company's market capitalization?

   a   A company's size based on the market value of its shares.

   b   A company's size based on its earnings.

   c   A company's size based on its sales.

3   The stock of which type of company is likely to be the least volatile?

   a   A small size company.

   b   A midsize company.

   c   A large size company.

4   To determine whether a stock is fairly valued, examine its:

   a   Market capitalization.

   b   Price/earnings ratio.

   c   Earnings-growth rate.

5   Which type of fund is likely to be the most volatile?

   a   A large-cap value fund.

   b   A mid-cap blend fund.

   c   A small-cap growth fund.

Worksheet

Look at a Morningstar report for one of the funds in your portfolio. What does its style box tell you about the types of companies your manager is investing in?

Find the style box placement for each of the funds in your portfolio. Are your funds scattered across the various squares of the style box, or do you have more than one fund that lands in any one square?

If you have more than one fund in a single square of the style box, do you have a good reason for holding both? Do the funds pursue the same or similar strategies?

Lesson 207: Examining a Stock Fund's Portfolio, Part Two

We've described the Morningstar style box as the "snapshot" of a fund's investment style. It's the best place to start if you're trying to uncover how a fund invests—but don't stop there. A handful of other portfolio statistics reveal additional insights into individual funds—information about a fund's risk and return potential that style boxes don't reveal.

Sector Weightings

Both Gabelli Value and MFS Mid Cap Value land in the mid-cap blend square of the style box, but the funds have very different biases. With 37% of its portfolio devoted to media stocks, the Gabelli fund is heavily exposed to the ups and downs of that sector. Meanwhile, MFS favors financial firms. Not surprisingly, these two funds have turned in different results. Gabelli's bet hasn't paid off this year—it's down nearly 3% through August 2004; MFS is chugging away, turning in a 4% gain.

Sector breakdowns can sometimes be confusing. Like a lot of industry watchers, Morningstar used to identify only the very broadest of sectors—"telecom," for example, or "technology." But not all technology stocks are the same, and some of them perform differently in different markets. So Morningstar has made a real effort to give investors more detail about their portfolios. For example, we now divide technology-related firms into hardware and software firms.

Sectors, subsectors, industries—what gives?

Welcome to one of our favorite portfolio statistics: sector weightings. Stocks fall into one of three "super" sectors—information, service, and manufacturing—which are subdivided into four sectors apiece, bringing the total number of sectors to 12. The information super-sector includes the software, hardware, media, and telecommunications sectors. In the service supersector, there are the health-care, consumer-services, business-services, and financial-services sectors. And finally, in the manufacturing supersector, there are consumer-goods, industrial-materials, energy, and utilities sectors. Morningstar calculates a fund's sector exposure based on the amount of assets it has in stocks in each sector. By knowing how heavily a fund invests in a given sector, you'll know how vulnerable it is to a downturn in that part of the market or how much sector risk it's taking on.

Morningstar's Sector Breakdown

⟳ Information Economy	☰ Service Economy	⌐ Manufacturing Economy
Software	Health Care	Consumer Goods
Hardware	Consumer Services	Industrial Materials
Telecommunications	Business Services	Energy
Media	Financial Services	Utilities

Twelve sectors are divided into three supersectors representing broader parts of the economy.

Average Market Capitalization

Okay, so average market capitalization is included in Morningstar's style box calculation. But you should examine it anyway because there are small-cap funds and there are really small-cap funds.

Take Brazos Microcap and AIM Opportunities, for example. Both land in the small-cap value portion of the style box. But despite its small-sounding name, Brazos sports an average market cap of $3.7 billion, while AIM's managers consistently buy tiny firms for a portfolio with an average market cap of $926 million. That's an enormous difference. That means that AIM will do well against other small-value funds when micro-caps are doing well in the market. Of course, it also lags when investors get nervous and flock to larger, more established firms. Investors who aren't aware of the fund's bias might evaluate the fund as good or bad without understanding the reason behind its performance.

Conversely, there's a difference between large-cap and really large-cap funds. Vanguard Growth Index, for instance, carried an average market capitalization of $40.9 billion in August 2004, while William Blair Growth clocked in at just $13 billion. While both are large-cap growth funds, the former fund will outperform the latter when giant-sized companies are leading the market. Conversely, the latter fund should one-up the former if smaller companies (well, small within the large-cap division) have the lead.

Price/Earnings and Price/Book Ratios

Price/earnings and price/book ratios, too, are included in the style box, but they are worthy of separate consideration. Just as there are degrees of market capitalizations, there are degrees of price multiples. White Oak Growth and Gabelli Growth both have "growth" in their names, but White Oak's P/E ratio of 37 is significantly higher than Gabelli's 21. That means that White Oak comes with more price risk than Gabelli Growth.

Number of Holdings

It's also important to know whether a fund holds 20 or 200 stocks. You'd expect a fund with fewer stocks to be more volatile than one with hundreds of names on hand. While that isn't always the case, it often is. Just as you need to be aware of funds that place a large portion of their assets in one or two sectors, you need to know if a fund places a large portion of assets in a small number of holdings.

Why focus is important	The number of stocks that a fund holds can often dictate its performance. The performance of funds with limited portfolios is often driven by the fates of just a few companies. After all, some of these firms can account for huge portions of the fund's assets. Investors beware: This risk isn't unique to daring, small-cap funds. There are plenty of focused large-value funds out there.

For example, Mosaic Midcap and Gabelli Asset are both mid-cap blend funds, yet the former generally owns less than 45 stocks while the latter stockpiles hundreds of names. Mosaic Midcap is taking on more risk—its performance is dependent on the success or failure of a much smaller number of stocks.

Turnover Rates

A fund's turnover rate represents the percentage of a fund's holdings that have changed over the past year, and it gives an idea of how long a manager holds on to a stock. Fund accountants calculate a fund's turnover rate by dividing its total sales or purchases (excluding cash), whichever is less, by its average monthly assets during the year. You can translate this math easily: A fund that trades 25% of its portfolio each year holds a stock for four years, on average.

Despite its seeming simplicity, turnover rates have their quirks. For instance, a dramatic change in the fund's asset base (the turnover ratio's denominator) can give a false impression of a fund's trading activity. If the manager doesn't change her trading pace, a fund's turnover ratio will decline as assets rise. Conversely, a shrinking asset base can inflate a fund's turnover ratio.

Turnover can give you a sense of a manager's trading activity, but don't read too much into a fund's turnover rate, particularly with bond funds. In general, buy-and-hold managers will have lower turnover rates than managers who trade on short-term factors. And generally, very high–turnover managers tend to practice aggressive strategies. With bond funds though, quite often managers employ cash-management strategies that inflate turnover rates. It's not uncommon to see turnover rates of 300% or more, even in funds that aren't particularly aggressive.

Turnover rate	The fund's turnover rate roughly approximates its trading habits. Morningstar doesn't calculate this figure; instead fund companies have to report it to the SEC, as it affects the offering's tax liabilities and trading costs. Generally, investors can assume that the turnover rate (which is published as percentage) can be interpreted as the percentage of the portfolio's holdings that have changed in the last year.

Fearless Facts

▶ Know your fund's industry loyalties. There's a good chance that your fund manager favors one or two sectors or industries. Any market watcher knows that different kinds of businesses—financial firms, tech companies, oil producers—enjoy different fates in different markets.

▶ Your fund's sector exposure is available on the fund company Web site and in shareholder reports. It's also updated in Morningstar's Fund Reports.

▶ Get the details on size. It's easy to identify large- and small-cap funds using the style box. But the fund's average market capitalization often tells you more than the style box can. The average market capitalization figure lets you know whether your fund manager is investing in small, established firms or in micro-cap companies—fledgling firms just stepping out into the market. Because micro-cap firms might suffer first and worst when investors get nervous, you should know if those firms are crammed into a portfolio.

▶ Delve into a fund's portfolio statistics for a better view of how it really invests. Portfolio ratios—including price/book and price/earnings measurements—are key to understanding the extent to which your fund manager is a bargain shopper or a luxury-brand hound. These ratios are available on Morningstar.com.

▶ Trading should matter to you—a lot. Turnover rates are a good way to understand surprising performance and they're one of the best ways to assess a fund's trading costs and what kinds of tax penalties you could face down the road. Turnover estimates are sometimes tough to find on fund Web sites and publicity materials, but firms are required to list them in shareholder reports. And—of course—you can always find them on Morningstar.com.

Quiz

1 Sector weightings tell you what?

Answers to this quiz can be found on page 237

   a   What a fund's investment style is.

   b   What industries your manager favors.

   c   How much price risk a fund is taking on.

2 Price/earnings multiples tell you what?

   a   How much sector risk a fund is taking on.

   b   How much price risk a fund is taking on.

   c   How much per-issue risk a fund is taking on.

3 A fund's number of holdings tells you what?

   a   How much sector risk a fund is taking on.

   b   How much price risk a fund is taking on.

   c   How much per-issue risk a fund is taking on.

4 A fund's turnover rate tells you what?

   a   How many managers a fund has had.

   b   Whether a manager likes high-growth companies.

   c   How frequently the manager trades the portfolio.

5 Which stock fund is likely the most volatile?

   a   A fund with a P/E of 25, 200 holdings, and a 20% turnover rate.

   b   A fund with a P/E of 30, 100 holdings, and a 50% turnover rate.

   c   A fund with a P/E of 35, 25 holdings, and a 200% turnover rate.

Worksheet

Examine the Morningstar report or shareholder report for one of the funds in your portfolio. Which sectors is your fund heavily invested in? Is it heavily concentrated in one or two sectors or diversified across the market? If the fund is concentrated in just a few sectors, do you have other funds that also invest heavily in those areas?

Find your fund's average market capitalization in its Morningstar report. How can you use this figure to determine its risk and possible return?

How many stocks does your fund hold? Are most of the funds that you own concentrated (with 50 holdings or less) or more diffuse? What are the advantages and disadvantages of each style?

What is your fund's turnover? Based on this turnover figure, can you tell whether you should hold the fund in a taxable or tax-sheltered account?

Diversify and Sleep Peacefully

Lesson 208: Why Diversify?

In this lesson, we'll cover what diversification is and what role it plays in building a mutual fund portfolio. Subsequent lessons in this level will discuss how to build a portfolio of mutual funds.

Diversification: What It Is

If you're having friends over for a barbecue, would you only serve meat? We may be a bunch of Midwesterners at Morningstar, but we're sophisticated enough to have heard of the four food groups and we'd expect more than just protein. Instead, you'd probably offer an assortment—some salad, maybe lemonade, and so on. In short, you'd diversify your table so that your guests would be satisfied.

Now consider investing. You want to own various types of funds so that your portfolio, as a group of investments, does well. Certain types of investments will do well at certain times while others won't. But if you have enough variety in your portfolio, it is pretty likely you'll always have something that is performing relatively well. Owning various types of funds can help reduce the volatility of your portfolio over the long term.

Let's say that you buy a value fund that owns a lot of cyclical stocks, or stocks that tend to do well when investors are optimistic about the economy. If that were your only fund, your returns wouldn't look very good during a recession. So you decide to diversify by finding a fund heavy in food and drug-company stocks, which tend to do relatively well during recessions. By owning the second fund, you limit your losses in an economic downturn. That is the beauty of diversification.

Diversification: What It Isn't.

Diversification isn't a magic bullet.

Having a diversified portfolio doesn't mean you'll never lose money. Diversification doesn't mean complete protection from short-term dips. Diversification does not guarantee that if one investment goes down another investment will go up—it isn't a seesaw.

August 1998 illustrated this point. It was an absolutely wretched time for investors; the average U.S. stock fund lost almost 17% that month. The average foreign-stock fund lost 14.4%. Funds that bought emerging-markets stocks were down twice that as Asia imploded. Real-estate funds tumbled 10.9%, while gold funds slid 22%. Even bond funds were in negative territory. Treasury bills were the only investment that made money for the month. The lesson: Because all sorts of investments can suffer at the same time, your only sure-fire protection against sudden losses is to put some of your assets in a money market fund.

Ways to Diversify

Diversification can occur at several different levels of your portfolio. Some of those levels are more important for mutual fund investors than others.

Diversifying Across Investments. Say you owned stock in a single company. If the company flourished, so would your investment. But if the company went bankrupt, you could lose all of your investment. To reduce your dependence on that single company, you buy stock in four or five other companies, as well. Even if one of your holdings sours, your overall portfolio won't suffer as much. By investing in a mutual fund, you're getting this same protection.

Diversifying by Asset Class. The three main asset classes are stocks, bonds, and cash. Some financial advisors contend that international stocks, real estate investment trusts, emerging-markets stocks, and the like are also asset classes—but the stocks, bonds, cash division is the most widely accepted. Adding bonds and cash (typically considered to be securities with maturities of one year or less) to a stock-heavy portfolio lowers your overall risk. Adding stocks to a bond- or cash-heavy portfolio increases your total-return potential. For most investors, it is wise to own a mix of all three. How you determine that mix depends on what your goals are and how long you plan to invest.

Diversifying by Subasset Classes. Within two of the three main asset classes—stocks and bonds—investors can choose several flavors of investments.

With stocks, for example, you may distinguish between U.S. stocks, foreign developed-market stocks, and emerging-markets stocks (typically considered to be stocks from emerging economies, including Latin America, the Pacific Rim, and Eastern Europe). Furthermore, within your U.S. stock allocation, you can have large-growth, large-value, small-growth, or small-value investments. You can also make investments in particular sectors of the market, such as real estate or technology. The possibilities for classification are endless and often overwhelming, even to experienced investors.

A seriously varied universe	Morningstar covers more than 50 subasset classes, which we refer to as categories, including everything from precious-metals funds to California municipal-bond funds to Japan-stock funds.

So what is the bottom line on diversification? Diversifying across investments and by asset class is crucial. Subasset class diversification is useful, but not everyone needs to own a government-bond fund, an international fund, a small-cap fund, a real-estate fund, and on and on. You should nonetheless consider the various ways that such investments might add diversity to your portfolio—and allow you to rest a little easier.

Fearless Facts

▶ **Minimize the shopping.** When it comes to diversifying, more isn't necessarily better. Plenty of investors build an entire U.S. stock market portfolio using a broad-market fund such as Vanguard Total Stock Market Index, which includes small-, medium-, and large-cap firms and combines cheap stocks and more pricey ones.

▶ **Remember that diversification is only half the job.** It can't protect you from losses, but it can mitigate the pain of market trouble that affects, say, primarily larger American companies.

▶ **There are three levels across which to diversify.**

1. **Across investments.** Remember Enron? Never devote all of your money to just a few stocks or bonds.

2. **Across broad asset classes.** In jittery markets, government bonds may be best and when disaster strikes, there's nothing like cash. But long term, you'll likely need some oomph in your portfolio, so participation in the equity markets is key.

3. **Across subasset classes.** A stock isn't a stock isn't a stock. American behemoth GE won't behave like Indian technology company Satyam Computer. You'll need to hold different kinds of firms to achieve different kinds of results.

Quiz

1 Which statement is false?

   a Diversification can improve your return over the short term.

   b Diversification can lower your volatility over the long term.

   c Diversification can ensure that you never lose money.

Answers to this quiz can be found on page 237

2 If you want surefire protection against short-term losses, buy:

   a A money market fund.

   b A real estate fund.

   c A large-cap fund.

3 Which is the least important type of diversification?

   a By investment.

   b By asset class.

   c By subasset class.

4 What does diversifying by asset class usually mean?

   a Owning multiple U.S. companies.

   b Owning a mix of stocks, bonds, and cash.

   c Owning a mix of growth, value, and international stocks.

5 You should own...

   a A small-company fund.

   b A bond fund.

   c Maybe neither.

Worksheet

Why is diversification so important to your portfolio?

Look back on your past mutual fund statements to find a month or
a quarter in which you lost money. Did you lose more than the S&P 500
Index during that period? Why or why not?

Examine your portfolio. Are you diversified? Does your fund portfolio
include exposure to different sectors and asset classes? Can you identify
any areas in which your portfolio might be lacking?

Diversifying your portfolio can often mean holding more and more
securities. Is this always a good idea? Why or why not?

Lesson 209: Building Your Mutual Fund Portfolio

There are no right answers.

Assembling a mutual fund portfolio is largely a matter of personal taste. How to invest depends on who is doing the investing. We would love to say that we know how to create the perfect portfolio—what funds you and everyone else should buy, and in what proportion, to meet each and every one of your goals. We would like to give you the model portfolio that will allow you and everyone else to retire at age 55, to buy that second home, to send your children to college. But we can't. There is just no one-size-fits-all answer. There is no one "correct" way to build a mutual fund portfolio.

Putting together a group of mutual funds is a matter of personal preference and personal goals. But there are some universals you should think about when choosing and combining funds.

Define Your Objectives and Priorities

This step is probably the toughest part of the investing process: sitting down to figure out why you're investing, what you're investing for, and how much money you'll need to reach that goal. Your goals and your risk tolerance should then determine what your portfolio looks like.

Keep in mind that your goals and your stomach might not agree. You may find, for example, that the idea of losing 20% in one quarter makes you nauseated, but you need to invest aggressively to have a shot at accumulating the return you'll need to reach your goal. If so, you will need to compromise by accepting the risk, changing the goal, or saving more.

Time plays a part, too. If your goal is to retire in 30 years, you might be more willing to put up with short-term ups and downs if it means reaching your long-term goal. If you suffer a loss, you have time to make up for it. But if your goal is just five years away, taking on more risk might not be a good idea because you have less time to make up for any losses.

Develop a Core

For each goal you have identified, you should have a core group of three or four funds that are proven performers. The bulk of your assets—typically 70% to 80%—should be invested in these core funds.

What are core holdings? They're the engines of your portfolio, the investments that you can count on to deliver year in and year out. Funds that fall into Morningstar's large-blend or large-value categories tend to be the best core investments for meeting your long-term goals. For shorter-term goals, consider short- or intermediate-term high-quality bond funds. Simplify the investing process by focusing on a few funds that can deliver what you want, and build your investment in those funds rather than adding other funds.

When looking for core funds, simple rules prevail. The more boring, the better; the goal is steady gains, not excitement. Look for funds with low fees, long-tenured managers, easily understandable strategies, moderate risk, and consistent performance.

The Role of Different Fund Categories in Your Portfolio

Core Role	Supporting Role	Specialty Role
Conservative Allocation	Bank Loan	Diversified Pacific/Asia
Foreign Large Blend	Convertibles	Emerging Markets Bond
Foreign Large Growth	Diversified Emerging Mkts	Japan Stock
Foreign Large Value	Europe Stock	Latin America Stock
Intermediate Government	Foreign Small/Mid Growth	Pacific/Asia ex-Japan Stk
Intermediate-Term Bond	Foreign Small/Mid Value	Specialty-Communications
Large Blend	High Yield Bond	Specialty-Financial
Large Growth	High Yield Muni	Specialty-Health
Large Value	Long Government	Specialty-Natural Res
Moderate Allocation	Long-Term Bond	Specialty-Precious Metals
Muni National Interm	Mid-Cap Blend	Specialty-Real Estate
Muni National Long	Mid-Cap Growth	Specialty-Technology
Muni Single State Interm	Mid-Cap Value	Specialty-Utilities
Muni Single State Long	Multisector Bond	World Bond
World Stock	Muni National Short	
	Short Government	
	Short-Term Bond	
	Small Blend	
	Small Growth	
	Small Value	
	Ultrashort Bond	
	World Allocation	

Limit How Much You Put Outside the Core

Noncore holdings are the stop-and-go funds that may juice up returns—funds that focus on a single industry or emerging markets, and funds run by managers who make large bets on particular holdings or on certain parts of the market. Small-cap funds could also fall into this category, simply because they tend to be more volatile than large-cap funds. Use noncore funds for diversification and growth potential. For instance, if your portfolio's core is made up of large-cap funds, you might want to add small-cap, international, or sector funds to the noncore portion of your portfolio for diversification. As we discussed in the previous lesson, a variety of funds improves the likelihood of at least one of your investments doing well at a given time.

For active investors, more on core	Set some minimum standards and choose funds that can withstand the test of time. Assess how the funds performed over good and bad markets and demand that managers deliver returns that land in the top 25% of their category for longer-term periods (five years or more).

Though you probably wouldn't want to put a significant portion of your portfolio in any one of these types of funds, they do allow for the possibility of extraordinary returns. Of course, they also generally carry a higher level of risk. But as long as you limit the riskier portion of your portfolio, you aren't likely to threaten the bulk of your nest egg. And for some people, core funds may be all they ever need.

Don't Worry about an Optimal Number of Funds

There is no ideal number of funds to own. We have seen fund junkies build 30-fund portfolios while other investors can be perfectly diversified owning just two or three funds.

What you should worry about is how diversified your portfolio is, regardless of how many funds are in it. If all of your funds were growth funds or were heavy on a particular sector, you could own dozens of funds and still not be adequately diversified. Conversely, a one-fund portfolio could be better diversified than a multifund portfolio, if that one fund were an index fund covering the entire stock market.

Before adding an investment to your portfolio for diversification's sake, run your portfolio through the Instant X-Ray tool on Morningstar.com. See how diversified your holdings really are. Then type in the investment that you want to buy and see what happens to your portfolio's overall profile. Did the new fund add the diversification that you had hoped it would? If not, ask yourself if you really need this new fund.

Consider Your Tax Situation

Are you investing in a tax-deferred account, such as an IRA or a 401(k)? If not, recognize that you'll be paying taxes on any income and realized gains from your funds. And remember, funds can be tax nightmares. So if you are investing in a taxable account, look for funds (particularly tax-managed funds) that generate strong aftertax results.

Fearless Facts

 Know yourself. You can't build a portfolio without articulating your goals. Ask some questions, such as:

1. What am I saving for?
2. When do I want it?
3. How much do I want?
4. How much am I willing to risk?

 When choosing a core holding, focus on steady, boring funds that regularly perform in the top half of their categories. These aren't hard to find. Morningstar's Analysts Picks lists are a good place to start.

 Know that core portfolio like the back of your hand. Once you identify holes in those core holdings (no Japanese stocks, perhaps? limited exposure to small, fast-growing companies?), you're ready to seek some specialty funds that might fill the gaps.

 Finally, be sure that your core holdings and your specialty funds are tax-efficient, especially if you're holding them in a taxable account.

Quiz

1 If you find that you need to take on a good deal more risk than you are comfortable with to reach a goal, which is not an option?

a	Take on the risk.
b	Adjust the goal.
c	Don't take on the risk and still plan to meet the goal.

Answers to this quiz can be found on page 238

2 Which type of fund makes a good core investment for most investors?

a	A large-cap blend fund.
b	An emerging-markets fund.
c	A technology fund.

3 Noncore funds can add what to a portfolio?

a	Spiced-up returns.
b	Diversification.
c	Both.

4 Everyone needs:

a	Core funds.
b	Noncore funds.
c	Tax-efficient funds.

5 Which is the better-diversified portfolio?

a	A portfolio with ten funds.
b	A portfolio with two funds.
c	Can't tell.

Worksheet

What are your goals? How much time are you giving yourself to reach those goals?

Given your goals, have you devoted enough of your portfolio to core funds? What characteristics make these core offerings rather than supporting funds?

What percentage of your portfolio will you allocate to noncore holdings? How will these noncore funds affect the risk/return profile of your portfolio? What do you gain by holding these? Are there any noncore funds you could eliminate to make more room for core-type funds?

Once you've set up your core group of funds, use Morningstar.com's Portfolio Manager to test-drive noncore holdings that you could use to diversify your portfolio. Did the addition of the noncore fund diversify your portfolio as you thought it would? Why or why not?

Lesson 210: Choosing an Index Fund

Index funds make low-maintenance investments. You don't need to worry about a manager changing his/her strategy: Because index funds rigorously track specific indexes, the manager doesn't have much say in the matter. Don't fear that your manager will leave for greener pastures, either: Index-fund managers aren't actively selecting stocks, so it doesn't matter much who is calling the shots. Finally, asset growth isn't an issue: Because indexing is a relatively low-turnover approach, index funds don't suffer under the weight of too many assets.

Choosing an index fund isn't such a snap, though. More than 250 index funds ply their trade in 27 different investment categories. To complicate matters, some investment categories (such as large-blend) have multiple index funds, many of them locked to a different benchmark. It's getting so you can't tell the players without a program.

To simplify the process of choosing an index fund that meets your needs, consider the following suggestions.

Know Which Index the Fund Follows

Vanguard 500 Index, Vanguard Total Stock Market, Domini Social Equity, and Schwab 1000 all land in the large-cap blend category. They all claim to be index funds. But their performance patterns have been very different over the past five years. What gives?

The funds may be large-blend, but they track different indexes.

Domini Social Equity focuses only on so-called socially responsible firms in the s&p 500, then adds about 150 companies that aren't in the index. (We'll cover socially responsible investing in an upcoming lesson.) Even though those companies are added for some extra diversification, the Domini index's technology, media, and telecommunications stakes are each at least 30% more than the s&p 500's, while the Domini index is much lighter than the s&p 500 in the utilities, industrials, and consumer-durables sectors.

Knowing what index a fund tracks gives you a handle on the risks and returns you can expect and how they differ from other index funds. If you are buying Domini Social Equity, for example, you'd better be a fan of Microsoft, which constituted nearly 6.0% of assets and was the fund's largest holding in June 2004. Meanwhile, Microsoft takes up a much more moderate 3.4% of Vanguard 500 Index, which tracks the s&p 500. Thanks to big positions in Microsoft and in growth sectors such as technology, media, and telecommunications, Domini Social Equity outpaced Vanguard 500 during the tech boom of the late 1990s, but tech's weakness hurt from 2000 through 2002.

Know Your Options

Thanks to the variety of index funds, you have much more flexibility than a decade ago, when tracking the s&p 500 was one of the only indexing options. Today, you can build a well-balanced portfolio made up entirely of index funds.

Here are some common indexes; there are various funds tracking these indexes, or some variation on them.

U.S. Stock Indexes		
Wilshire Large Growth Screens 750 largest U.S. stocks for sales growth and other growth indicators.	**Wilshire Midcap Growth** Screens 501st to 1,250th largest U.S. stocks, following same criteria as Wilshire Large Growth.	**Wilshire Small Growth** Screens 751st to 2,500th largest U.S. stocks, following same criteria as Wilshire Large Growth.
Standard & Poor's 500 500 of the largest U.S. stocks, both value and growth.	**Standard & Poor's Midcap 400** 501st to 900th largest U.S. stocks, both value and growth.	**Russell 2000** 1,001st to 3,000th largest U.S. stocks, both value and growth.
Wilshire Large Value Screens 750 largest U.S. stocks for lowest P/E and P/B ratios, and highest yields.	**Wilshire Midcap Value** Screens 501st to 1,250th largest U.S. stocks, following same criteria as Wilshire Large Value.	

International Indexes		
MSCI World Captures 60% of every developed country's market capitalization and industry sectors, including the United States	**MSCI EAFE** Captures 60% of market cap and industries for 20 countries in Europe, Australia, and the Far East, excluding the United States.	**MSCI Emerging Markets** Applies MSCI criteria to markets identified as emerging by in-house guidelines.

Bond Indexes		
Lehman Bros. Long-Term Govt/Credit Includes Treasury, agency, and corporate bonds with face values of more than $100 million and maturities of at least 10 years.	**Lehman Bros. Interm-Term Govt/Credit** Uses same criteria as Lehman Brothers Long-Term, but includes bonds with maturities of at least one year and less than 10 years.	**Lehman Bros. Aggregate** Captures intermediate-term government bonds, mortgage securities, and investment-grade corporate issues.

Know the Tax Effects

One of the most common myths about indexing is that all index funds are tax-efficient. Funds that buy the biggest stocks, such as Vanguard 500, do boast terrific tax efficiency: As of August 2004, Vanguard 500's shareholders had kept over 90% of their pretax earnings from the past 10 years. That's because stocks that drop out of the large-cap S&P 500 usually are pretty small players in the index (most companies drop out of the index precisely because they've become too small)—after the 225th stock, none accounts for more than 0.10% of the index. When index funds sell these smaller positions, they don't reap sizable taxable gains.

Don't expect tax efficiency from funds tracking other indexes, though. Shareholders of Vanguard Small Cap Index, for example, haven't had such an easy ride. Funds following smaller-cap indexes have to sell stocks that have grown too large to remain in the small-company index; because those are also the funds' largest positions, selling them means realizing large capital gains, which then have to be distributed to shareholders.

You can find out how tax efficient an index fund is by checking out the fund's Fund Report on Morningstar.com.

Know the Costs

Another common assumption about indexing is that all index funds are cheap. Because they don't demand the resources of active management, they certainly ought to be. But some index funds charge surprisingly high annual expenses. Consider this: Green Century Equity, one of the priciest no-load large-blend index funds at the end of 2002, takes a huge 1.5% bite out of your investment every year. That is awfully steep when you consider that the average large-blend index fund's expense ratio is 0.60%. And even that looks pretty stiff compared with Vanguard 500's modest 0.18% fee.

Of course, you might willingly pay more for some index funds, such as Domini Social Equity (0.92%), because you want the socially responsible screens it applies in deciding which companies to include in its index. But all things being equal, cheaper is better.

Fearless Facts

▶ When shopping for index funds, know what you're getting. The benchmark the fund is trying to beat will be identified on the offering's Web site and in its shareholder reports.

▶ Be wary of funds that track a "proprietary benchmark" or an "in-house index." What that really means is that the fund company has put together its own index, one that isn't public. Of course, it's harder to prove your fund's performance against this benchmark— and there's no way to check up on the firm when they say they've beaten it!

▶ You can track the progress of the indexes we've listed on many financial Web sites, in the newspaper, or on Morningstar.com.

▶ Always, always remember to keep track of the costs you're incurring. Index funds shouldn't be charging much.

Quiz

1   Which is an advantage of index funds?

a	There aren't many of them, so it's easy to choose one.
b	They're low maintenance.
c	They're all incredibly tax efficient.

Answers to this quiz can be found on page 239

2   Which statement is true?

a	All index funds in the large-blend category follow the S&P 500.
b	All index funds in the large-cap blend category are cheap.
c	Index funds in the large-cap blend category can follow different indexes.

3   Which type of index fund is bound to be the least tax-friendly?

a	Small-company index funds.
b	Large-company index funds.
c	S&P 500 index funds.

4   Which statement is false?

a	You can build a portfolio entirely of index funds.
b	Because index funds don't involve managers actively choosing stocks, their management fees should be low.
c	Index funds are all cheap.

5   The Russell 2000 Index includes:

a	Large U.S. stocks.
b	Small U.S. stocks.
c	Bonds.

Worksheet

What is an index fund? How can you use an index fund in your portfolio?

Do you have any index funds in your portfolio? If so, which index does your fund track, and what types of companies does it buy?

Use the list of indexes within the lesson to identify a good benchmark for three funds in your portfolio. How has your funds' performance stacked up against the indexes you've chosen for them?

What is the most important characteristic to look for when considering an index fund? Why?

Lesson 211: SRI Funds

No politics. No religion. We're taught to avoid delicate subjects at the dining room table.

There's no longer any need to avoid these issues when it comes to investing, though. Now, investors can cling to their values using socially responsible funds. Very broadly, socially responsible investing (SRI) weaves values-based, nonfinancial criteria into the investment process.

But that definition is pretty broad. The SRI label can apply to various, even contradictory, investing strategies. For example, Citizens Value screens out firms that are inhospitable to gay and lesbian employees, while the Christian-oriented Timothy Plan Small-Cap Value Fund avoids companies that provide domestic-partner benefits.

Despite the complexity, though, there are really just five basic questions you need to answer when looking for an SRI fund.

What Issues Are Most Important to Me?

Before getting bogged down in reams of information about different SRI funds, examine your own values. Which issues are driving you to become a socially conscious investor? Do you simply want to avoid investing in alcohol and tobacco stocks? Are you especially concerned about the environment? Are issues of workplace diversity critical to you? Do you want to avoid weapons makers?

Once you've identified the issues that mean the most to you, decide if you'd like a religious or a secular fund. The largest and best-known SRI funds, such as Domini Social Equity, Pax World Balanced, the Citizens funds, and the Calvert funds, are secular funds. They usually avoid weapons makers and nuclear-power, alcohol, and tobacco firms. In addition, many secular SRI funds look for those companies with the best environmental, human-rights, and workplace-diversity records.

SRI sources to know	Social Investment Forum:	http://www.socialinvest.org
	Amana Funds:	http://www.amanafunds.com
	Calvert Funds:	http://www.calvert.com
	Citizens Funds	http://www.citizensfunds.com
	Domini Funds:	http://www.domini.com
	Noah Fund:	http://www.noahfund.com
	PaxWorld Funds:	http://www.paxworld.com

The Social Investment Forum now lists more than 80 socially responsible funds on its site. New players include funds from the Sierra Club (www.sierraclubfunds.com) and from the Women's Equity Mutual Fund (http://www.womens-equity.com).

A growing number of religious offerings cater to an assortment of denominations. The MMA Praxis funds are designed for Mennonite investors; the Catholic Values and Aquinas funds serve Catholics; the Amana funds were created for Islamic investors; and the Timothy, Noah, and Shepherd Values funds serve conservative Christians. The majority of religious funds avoid alcohol, gambling, and pornography stocks, but their screens vary widely in other ways. For example, because of an Islamic principle against usury (interest), the Amana funds don't invest in bonds or many financial stocks.

How Does a Fund Screen Its Investments?

Once you decide which screens are most important to you, it's time to find the closest match. You might start by looking at Web sites that provide details on socially responsible investing. The most complete Web site of how SRI funds screen companies is the Social Investment Forum: www.socialinvest.org.

Accurate information about a fund family's screening efforts is also often available on the firm's Web site. Moreover, prospectuses and annual reports carry basic information about the types of social screens that the funds use. SRI customer-service representatives should also be able to answer your questions.

Finally, examine a recent portfolio of any SRI fund you're seriously considering. Sure, a fund may say it uses environmental screens, but are those screens stringent enough for you? For example, Neuberger Berman Socially Responsive takes a relative approach to screening. That is, the managers look for the companies in each industry with the best workplace and environmental records. That means, however, that the fund owns oil-exploration company Newfield Exploration. Investors seeking stellar environmental records may not be that comfortable owning even the most socially responsible oil-exploration firm.

Is This Fund Involved in Shareholder Activism and Community Investment?

No corporation will clear all socially responsible hurdles. A company may have an excellent environmental record, but it may not provide the best working environment for its minority employees. If SRI funds demanded perfection from every company they owned, they would never buy anything.

Thus, some fund families, including Domini and Calvert, use shareholder activism to challenge the policies of some of those companies they do own. Because shareholders own the company, they can push for it to change. Other times, funds simply engage the firm in a discussion, quietly pressuring the company to make alterations to the policies it considers unpalatable. To find out if a fund you're considering engages in shareholder activism, visit its Web site or call the company itself.

Is This a Good Investment?

Just because you want to invest with your heart doesn't mean you should risk losing your shirt. On average, SRI funds have performed at least as well as non-socially screened funds. There are some poorly performing SRI funds out there, however, and you should avoid those as you would any bad fund.

Also, find out how expensive the fund is. You'll probably have to pay more for your socially screened funds. That's because such funds are typically smaller than their nonscreened peers and smaller funds tend to have higher expenses. Higher expenses may also reflect the additional research required to determine whether or not a company passes the fund's social screens.

SRI funds typically aren't cheap. Although a couple of low-cost alternatives, such as Vanguard Calvert Social Index and TIAA-CREF Social Choice, have emerged in recent years, many SRI funds are still burdened with high expenses.	Beware

How Do These Funds Work in My Portfolio?

Do you want an entire portfolio of funds that match your values, or are you comfortable with just one or two SRI offerings? There are socially responsible funds available in all major asset classes, although they're not equal in quality or quantity. SRI funds focusing on U.S. companies are the most plentiful. However, there are only a handful of SRI bond and international funds.

If you can't find enough suitable funds to build an all-SRI portfolio, you might simply choose one SRI fund to serve as a good large-cap core holding. After all, the largest companies are likely to have the biggest impact on the issues you care about, so why not focus on the big guys? There are a number of respectable large-cap funds available to socially conscious investors, including Vanguard Calvert Social Index, Domini Social Equity, Pax World, Noah, Amana Income, and Citizens Core Growth.

Fearless Facts

▶ Before you invest, figure out what companies you feel good about (or, more easily, identify the firms you don't want to support).

▶ Remember that there's a difference between funds that use an SRI strategy—avoiding certain companies—and funds engaged in shareholder activism—using their shareholder clout to pressure companies to improve their corporate citizenship. Many funds do both, of course.

▶ Before you buy, make sure you know the answers to the following questions:

1. How does the fund screen firms?
2. Does it engage in shareholder activism?
3. What role will this fund play in my overall portfolio?
4. How has it performed over the long haul?
5. How risky has it been over the long haul?
6. How much does it cost?

Quiz

1   Socially responsible funds:

a   All buy stocks of companies that provide domestic-partner benefits.

b   All avoid stocks of companies with poor human-rights records.

c   May screen companies on different values; there's no one SRI approach.

Answers to this quiz can be found on page 239

2   An SRI fund:

a   Would never own an oil company.

b   Might own an oil company.

c   Would always own an oil company.

3   Shareholder activism is a key for:

a   Some SRI funds.

b   All SRI funds.

c   No SRI funds.

4   The average SRI fund's costs are:

a   About the same as the average non-SRI fund's.

b   Less than the average non-SRI fund's.

c   More than the average non-SRI fund's.

5   Which statement is false?

a   It's easy to build a well-diversified, high-quality portfolio made up only of SRI funds.

b   There aren't as many good SRI bond or international funds as there are good SRI funds investing in U.S. stocks.

c   SRI funds can use dramatically different criteria.

Worksheet

Is socially responsible investing of interest to you? Would you be willing to pay a higher expense ratio for a fund that embodies your values? Why or why not?

If socially responsible investing is of interest to you, are there any particular types of companies you'd like your fund to avoid? Are secular or religious concerns more important to you?

How is shareholder activism different from socially responsible screening? Is either process more or less appealing to you?

Why might SRI funds tend to skimp on certain parts of the market, such as energy or industrial companies? Which industries do you think SRI funds might be heavy on?

Fearlessly Select International and Bond Funds

Lesson 212: Choosing an International Fund, Part One

By September 2002, U.S. investors had poured $370 billion into funds that primarily buy stocks of foreign companies.

What's the attraction? Alluring returns, for one. In 1999, for example, the average foreign-stock fund gained a phenomenal 44%, while the S&P 500 rose only about half as much. What's more, foreign investing offers sought-after diversification. As we discussed in **Lesson 208: Why Diversify?**, if you own a variety of investments, chances are you'll always have a hand in something that's performing well.

Unless you understand how to evaluate these funds, though, investing abroad can be pretty harrowing. The key to smart foreign-fund investing comes down to looking beyond returns and Morningstar ratings and understanding how your fund invests. By doing so, you will be able to set reasonable expectations for the investment and uncover its hidden risks—and avoid surprises. Start by asking the two questions that appear on the following pages. You can find most of the answers to these questions on the Morningstar Fund Report, on the fund family's Web site, or in the fund's shareholder report.

Does the Fund Own Emerging-Markets Stocks?

At the beginning of 2004, many of the best-performing international funds kept a good slug of their assets in emerging-markets stocks, or stocks of companies domiciled in smaller or less-developed markets, such as India, Chile, or Russia.

❶

Developing, third world, emerging—what's with the lingo?	In the past few years, the language used to identify countries that show up in emerging-markets portfolios has changed quite a bit. Nowadays, fund managers talk about industrializing countries, often referring to countries such as India or China; adjusted countries, referring to countries in Latin America that have adopted international bank and accounting standards; and emerging Europe, referring to the Czech Republic, Poland, and Hungary.

Owning emerging-markets stocks has its benefits. First, they can generate robust returns: The MSCI Emerging Markets Index soared a phenomenal 64% in 1999, fueled by the Asian tech boom that took much of the investing public by surprise. Emerging-markets stocks also add more diversity to a U.S. portfolio than stocks from many of the more-developed international markets, such as Germany and the United Kingdom, do. That's because the returns of the U.S. market and other developed markets tend to move in tandem.

There's a price for emerging-markets stocks' exhilarating highs and diversification, though: the threat of steep losses. In June 1998, for example, the MSCI Emerging Markets Index was in a free fall: It had shed 19% in the preceding six months. The developing world suffered currency collapses and soaring inflation, and investors' returns suffered. If oscillating fortunes make you sweat, limit your search to funds that are light on emerging-markets stocks.

If you're trying to avoid emerging markets, you'll need to be vigilant; after all, most diversified international funds nibble at emerging-markets stocks. In fact, the average fund in the foreign-stock category held more than 10% of its assets in emerging-markets names at the end of 2001, a bit less in 2002, and a bit more over the next two years. Your best bet is to find out which countries a fund frequents. Funds that go shopping in Europe, the U.S., and Japan are focusing on developed markets. But if you see a number of companies from countries in Latin America or the Pacific Region, you'll know that the fund is venturing into emerging markets.

The folks at JP Morgan have put together an index that tracks emerging markets. This is by no means an exhaustive list, but it's a good clue to what countries most fund managers are considering when they talk about venturing into emerging markets.

What really counts as emerging?

Does It Concentrate in a Specific Region or Country?

While you are examining a fund's country exposure, get a feel for whether the fund prefers a few markets or a particular region, or whether it casts a wider net. Morningstar clumps international funds that focus on a single region into one of the following regional categories: Europe stock, Latin America stock, Japan stock, Pacific/Asia stock, and Pacific/Asia ex-Japan stock.

However, funds can overweight particular countries or regions and still land in the broad foreign-stock category because they have enough variety among their holdings to avoid being classified as regional funds. For example, Tocqueville International Value and Longleaf Partners International both housed more than 35% of their assets in Japan in mid-2002. The average foreign-stock fund, by comparison, held less than 20% in Japan.

Note that a good dose of any single region or country (especially volatile Japan) can deliver uneven results. In spite of a stellar performance in the bear markets of 2001 and 2002, Japan-heavy Tocqueville International Value also lost 31% of its value in 1997 and another 20% in 2000. To stay off the return trampoline, find funds that own stocks from a wide variety of markets.

Fearless Facts

▶ International funds have been a go-to source for diversification for years. Even as global markets become increasingly synchronized, international funds can offer some real respite from the ups and downs of U.S. markets.

▶ International funds have the potential to be quite volatile on their own, so it helps to have a thorough understanding of your international fund manager's style.

▶ Before internationalizing your portfolio, make sure that you check up on the following:

1. How often does the manager shop in emerging markets?
2. Which countries does the manager favor?

Quiz

1   Why own an international fund?

a	For the often good returns.
b	For the diversification.
c	Both.

Answers to this quiz can be found on page 240

2   To choose a good international fund:

a	Rely solely on Morningstar ratings.
b	Look only at past returns.
c	Understand how the fund invests.

3   Which of the following is not true about emerging-markets stocks?

a	They are low risk.
b	They can offer stunning returns.
c	They offer great diversification.

4   To find out if a fund owns a lot of emerging-markets stocks:

a	Find out what its Morningstar category is.
b	Examine what countries most of its stocks hail from.
c	Look at its star rating.

5   Which would likely be most volatile?

a	A diversified foreign-stock fund with 10% of its assets in emerging-markets stocks.
b	A diversified emerging-markets fund.
c	A Latin American fund.

Worksheet

We have a huge and developed stock market right here in the U.S. What are the reasons an investor might consider an international fund for a portion of his or her portfolio?

If you have a foreign-stock fund, take a look at its report on Morningstar.com. Click on the Portfolio tab (in the lefthand column of your fund's report). Is your fund investing in developed markets such as Western Europe and Japan, or emerging markets such as India or Chile? Or is it investing in a combination of the two?

Do you think heavy regional or country exposure is a good idea for your investment needs? Why or why not?

Lesson 213: Choosing an International Fund, Part Two

As you learned in **Lesson 212: Choosing an International Fund, Part One**, examining the countries that an international fund invests in is central to understanding whether the fund is right for you. If sharp market movements make you nervous, investing in a fund that concentrates just on Latin America or Asia's emerging markets probably isn't the best idea for you.

But the countries in which a fund invests constitute only one factor contributing to an international fund's returns and volatility. Two other elements—the manager's investment style and currency-hedging policy—play equally important roles. Thus, you have two additional questions to ask before buying an international fund.

What Is Its Style?

A few years ago, style wasn't an issue for foreign-stock funds. Most funds bought reasonably priced stocks of the world's largest companies. After all, international-investing pioneers such as Sir John Templeton and the managers at Scudder had profited for decades by using such strategies. In the 1990s, though, Janus and American Century met with great success when they began applying the growth-focused strategies they used at home to investing abroad. Their styles were still novel among foreign-stock investors.

The issue of investment style doesn't end with the choice between value and growth. It also involves the question of the size—otherwise known as market capitalization—of the stocks in which a fund invests. To determine an international fund's investment style, consult its Morningstar style box, which you can find on the Fund Report.

Why size matters when shopping abroad	We've said that smaller-cap foreign companies usually offer more diversification than larger-cap firms. Very small firms are often dependent mainly on local business and will be insulated from the ups and downs of American markets.

A fund's investment style will have a direct impact on its risk level. If ups and downs make you queasy, steer clear of funds that emphasize small foreign companies because they tend to be more volatile than large-cap players. (Just like volatile emerging-markets stocks, though, foreign small-cap stocks generally do a better job of diversifying a U.S. portfolio than foreign large-cap stocks do.) And the easiest way to get exposure to both large-value and large-growth foreign stocks is through a large-blend foreign fund.

What Is Its Currency-Hedging Policy?

When fund managers buy foreign stocks, they're also effectively buying the foreign currency that the stock is denominated in. So a foreign stock's return is really a combination of two things: the performance of the stock itself and the performance of the country's currency versus the U.S. dollar.

Let's take an example. Say you buy a Japanese stock, Sony. The value of the stock itself rises 10%. But the yen (Japan's currency) falls 15% against the U.S. dollar. As a U.S. investor, you've lost money on that investment because even though the stock price has risen, the currency's value has fallen. What if the yen rises 10% instead? Then you've doubled your return because you get the 10% rise in the stock's price and the 10% rise in the currency.

Managers can own foreign stocks and, with a little work, eliminate their exposure to foreign currencies. They do that by hedging their foreign currencies—trading in their foreign currencies for U.S. dollars.

When a fund buys a foreign company and hedges its currency exposure, it's actually involved in two very different areas. One is the equity market, in which the fund's traders are actually buying shares of various companies. The other is the global currency market, in which the fund's traders are signing contracts to buy (or sell) foreign currency at some point in the future—usually about six months out. In doing so, they are guaranteeing the fund a certain exchange rate, one they can count on, one designed to protect you, their investor, against currency volatility. Their activities have practically nothing to do with the portfolio manager's decision to buy or sell French Company A or British Company B.

Hedging: How is it done?

Let's go back to our example. You buy Sony, but hedge your currencies by selling Japanese yen and buying U.S. dollars. Sony's stock rises 10% and the yen falls 10% against the dollar. Because you hedged your currency exposure, whether the yen rises or falls doesn't have any effect on your investment.

Most studies indicate that hedging currencies has only a minimal effect on returns over very long time periods. But over shorter spans, hedging can make quite a difference in a fund's performance. The managers of Putnam International Growth, for example, claim they added two percentage points of return in 1997 by moving out of falling currencies and into the rising U.S. dollar.

If you can't quite understand why a foreign fund is behaving the way it is, chances are the fund manager is doing something with currencies. To avoid the unexpected behavior that can accompany mistimed currency plays, you can favor funds with strict hedging policies—those that never hedge or those that always do. Consult a fund's shareholder report to find out whether or not it hedges its currencies. If this information isn't available in the shareholder report, call the fund company and ask.

Fearless Facts

▶ When selecting among international funds, understanding your own risk tolerance is key. Some international managers have more daring strategies than their domestic counterparts.

▶ International funds that focus on smaller companies help diversify portfolios that are heavy on large-cap U.S. stocks, but foreign small-cap funds also have the potential for a fair amount of volatility.

▶ Before internationalizing your portfolio, make sure that you check up on the following:

1. What kinds of companies does the manager like? It's easy to focus on one style when investing abroad. Be sure to know if you're getting a growth-heavy portfolio or a value-laden one, a small-cap offering or a large-cap fund.

2. What kind of currency exposure do you want? What kind are you getting? If you're looking for true international exposure, you may wish to shoulder the risk that comes along with non-dollar investing. If, however, you'd like foreign-stock exposure without all of the currency fluctuations, a fund that regularly hedges will be your best bet.

Quiz

1 International small-cap funds are:

a	Better performers than international large-cap funds.
b	Poorer performers than international large-cap funds.
c	More volatile than international large-cap funds.

Answers to this quiz can be found on page 241

2 International funds:

a	Can invest in value or growth stocks.
b	All invest in reasonably priced stocks of large companies.
c	Buy only small-company stocks.

3 For a U.S. investor, the return on a foreign stock is:

a	The return of the stock itself.
b	The return of the currency.
c	The return of the stock itself and the currency in which it's denominated.

4 You buy shares of Britain's Glaxo. The stock falls 5%, but the pound (Britain's currency) gains 10% against the dollar. As an unhedged U.S. investor, you:

a	Lost money.
b	Made money.
c	Broke even.

continued...

5   You buy shares of Britain's Glaxo. The stock falls 5%, but the pound gains 10% against the dollar. You've hedged your currency back into U.S. dollars. You have:

a   Lost money.

b   Made money.

c   Broke even.

Worksheet

Examine the prospectus of one of your international funds. What does the fund manager look for? Stocks that are trading cheaply? Fast-growing small companies? Does your foreign fund's strategy overlap with any of your U.S. stock funds' approaches? Why might that be a problem?

Examine your international fund's portfolio. Do you recognize any of your fund's stocks? How could the fact that these companies earn revenues from the U.S. affect the diversification benefit you derive from the fund?

Based on its holdings and style box, does your foreign fund fit the "core" designation? Why or why not?

See if you can find information about your fund's currency-hedging policy in its shareholder report. If not, call the fund company and ask whether it hedges its currency exposure all of the time, some of the time, or never. Do you think its currency-hedging policy will increase its risk, decrease it, or have no effect?

Lesson 214: Bond Funds, Part One

Glazed eyes. Gaping mouths.

Bond talk is generally considered a sure-fire way to put your dinner companions to sleep. We're convinced that this is largely because people don't really understand the basics of bonds and like everyone—yes, everyone, including the media and a lot of so-called market "experts"—they're terrified by the fixed-income world.

In the next two lessons, we'll quell that terror, detailing all you need to know before choosing your first—and perhaps only—bond fund.

What Bonds Are

If you're going to choose a bond fund, the harsh truth is that you need to know what a bond is. When you buy a stock, you become part owner of the company. When you buy a bond, you are making a loan; you are simply lending money to the company (or, in the case of Treasury bonds, to the government). Your loan lasts a certain period of time—until the date that the bond reaches maturity. In the meantime, you can typically expect dividend payments (commonly known as coupons) as interest on the loan. Thus, the essential issues for bond investing will be the bond's maturity and how confident you are that the business or government can actually repay the loan.

Understanding Interest-Rate Risk

Two forces govern the performance of bonds and bond funds: interest-rate sensitivity (or duration) and credit quality. Let's start with rate sensitivity.

Is it really so simple?	Sadly, no. One of the biggest mistakes investors make is to assume that when rates go up, bonds of a similar credit quality will lose the same amount. Not so. Usually, the longer a bond's life span, or maturity, the more it's affected by interest-rate changes.

Bond prices move in the opposite direction of interest rates. When rates fall, bond prices rise. When rates rise, bond prices fall. To determine how dramatic a fund's rises and falls might be, check out its duration.

Duration—or interest-rate risk—boils down to the three risk factors of bonds: maturity, the cash flows from coupons, and current interest rates. Sound confusing? Think of a bond as a pro-basketball player's contract. In negotiating his first contract, a top draft pick wants a salary that will stay competitive with what's offered in the NBA. Looking at different contract proposals, he'll consider the length of a contract (its maturity), the salary (the coupons or cash flow), and wages across the league (current interest rates).

Suppose the player is offered an average five-year contract at $1 million a year. He likes the cash flow, but he's nervous about the long-term commitment. If he takes the five-year contract and the average NBA salary spikes up, he'll be earning a lower salary than average in the last years of the deal, and a lower salary is more likely to become noncompetitive than a higher one. Duration expresses these trade-offs as a kind of risk measure that investors can use for comparison purposes.

One of the nonintuitive aspects of duration is that it's expressed in years, just like maturity. But duration isn't nearly as concrete a concept as maturity. Take a bond with a maturity of 11 years and a duration of 8.5 years. At the end of 11 years, we know that something happens—the bond is paid off. But what happens after 8.5 years? Nothing, really.

Bonds that sport low coupon rates are more vulnerable to changes in interest rates. In fact, you'll see the price of a low-coupon bond bounce around a lot as the interest-rate environment changes.

Also vulnerable to interest rates

Duration is a useful abstraction, though. The higher a bond's duration, the more it responds to changes in interest rates. If a bond fund has a duration of five years, you can expect it to gain 5% if interest rates fall by one percentage point, and to lose 5% if interest rates rise by one percentage point. And that bond fund with a duration of 8.5 years? We know it's more volatile, and more vulnerable to interest-rate changes, than the bond fund with a duration of five years.

At Morningstar, we're fans of funds with short- and intermediate-term durations—between three and five years. They're just less volatile than longer-duration funds and offer nearly as much return. Ibbotson Associates, an investment research company, reports that intermediate-term government bonds were both less volatile and better-performing than long-term government bonds between 1925 and 1995. That's quite a combination.

Understanding Credit Risk

Interest-rate risk is but one risk that bond funds face. The other, credit risk, involves the fund's credit quality. Credit quality simply measures the ability of an issuer to repay its debts.

Think of it this way. If your no-good brother-in-law who hasn't held a job in six years wants to borrow $50 from you, you would probably wonder if you'd ever see that $50 again. You'd be far more likely to loan money to your super-responsible kid sister who just needs a little emergency cash. The same dynamic occurs between companies and investors. Investors eagerly loan money to well-established companies that seem likely to repay their debts, but they think twice about loaning to firms without a solid track record or that have fallen on hard times.

Judgments about a firm's ability to pay its debts are encapsulated in a credit rating. Credit-rating firms, such as Moody's and Standard & Poor's, closely examine a firm's financial statements to get an idea of whether a company is closest to being a no-goodnik or a debt-paying good citizen. They then assign a letter grade to the company's debt: AAA indicates the highest credit quality and D indicates the lowest.

So if you hold a bond rated AAA, odds are very good that you'll collect all of your coupons and principal. Indeed, bonds rated AAA, AA, A, and BBB are considered investment-grade, meaning that it's pretty likely the company that issued the bonds will repay its debts. Bonds rated BB, B, CCC, CC, and C are non-investment-grade, or high-yield, bonds. That means there's a good chance that the bond issuer will renege on its obligations, or default. In fact, D, the lowest grade, is reserved for bonds that are already in default.

Of course, you probably don't want a bond that may not pay its promised coupons and principal. The main purpose in owning a bond, after all, is getting your hands on its income. So if you're bond shopping, you're not going to pick up a lower-rated bond just for the heck of it. You need some sort of incentive. That incentive comes in the form of higher yields. All other things being equal, the lower a bond's credit quality, the higher its yield. That's why you can find a high-yield bond fund with a yield of 9% or more, while many investment-grade bond funds offer yields around 4%. Because investment-grade issuers are more likely to meet their obligations, investors trade higher income for greater certainty.

Credit quality affects more than just a bond's yield, though; it can also affect its value. Specifically, lower-rated bonds tend to drop in value when the economy is in recession or when investors think the economy is likely to fall into a recession. Recessions usually mean lower corporate profits and thus less money to pay bondholders. If an issuer's ability to repay its debt looks a little shaky in a healthy economy, it will be even more suspect in a recession. High-yield bond funds usually drop in value when investors are worried about the economy.

Fearless Facts

▶ Bonds are just loans that you make to a company or government. The legal structure surrounding firms in the U.S. ensures that if a firm goes bankrupt, they have to pay their creditors (their lenders) back before they reimburse their stockholders. That's partly why bonds are often seen as "less risky" than stocks.

▶ You can think of interest-rate risk as the problem of opportunity cost: If you buy a bond with a longer maturity now, while rates are low, you're shouldering the possibility that rates could change down the line.

▶ You can think of credit risk, however, in much the same way you think about your equity holdings. Credit ratings reflect the rating agency's opinion as to whether or not the company to which you lent money will implode or go bankrupt.

Quiz

1   **If interest rates rise, bond prices:**

Answers to this quiz can be found on page 241

a	Rise.
b	Fall.
c	Stay the same.

2   **Duration measures a bond's:**

a	Interest-rate sensitivity.
b	Credit quality.
c	Yield.

3   **Which bond fund is taking on the most interest-rate risk?**

a	The fund with a five-year duration and an average credit quality of B.
b	The fund with a six-year duration and an average credit quality of A.
c	The fund with a seven-year duration and an average credit quality of AAA.

4   **Which bond fund is taking on the most credit risk?**

a	The fund with a five-year duration and an average credit quality of B.
b	The fund with a six-year duration and an average credit quality of A.
c	The fund with a seven-year duration and an average credit quality of AAA.

5   **High-yield bonds will do poorly when:**

a	Interest rates fall.
b	The economy does well.
c	There's a recession.

Worksheet

What kinds of risk do you face when you're investing in bonds? How are these risks different from the risks you shoulder when you invest in stock funds?

Why do you think that bond returns aren't as high as stock returns?

When you buy bond funds, what are the three most important things to focus on?

If you own a bond fund, go on the fund company's Web site or to Morningstar.com to find out what its yield is. If you wanted to obtain a higher yield than your fund is currently paying out, what additional risks would you have to take?

Lesson 215: Bond Funds, Part Two

In **Lesson 214: Bond Funds, Part One**, we introduced the two drivers of bond performance: duration and credit quality. In this course, we examine what Morningstar brings to the table: the fixed-income (a common term for bonds because they pay a fixed dividend to bondholders) style box and our tips for smart bond-fund buying.

Morningstar's Fixed-Income Style Box

The fixed-income style box is a nine-square box that gives you a visual snapshot of a fund's credit quality and duration. The style box allows investors to quickly gauge the risk exposure of their bond fund.

The horizontal axis of the fixed-income style box displays a fund's interest-rate sensitivity, as measured by the average duration of all the bonds in its portfolio. Morningstar breaks interest-rate sensitivity into three groups: short, intermediate, and long. In previous lessons, we explained that short-term bond funds are the least affected by interest-rate movements and thus the least volatile; long-term funds are the most volatile. Taxable-bond funds (as opposed to municipal-bond funds, which are protected from taxes) with average durations of less than 3.5 years fall in the short-term column; those with average durations longer than six years fall in the long-term column. Everything else is intermediate. (The cutoffs for municipal-bond funds are slightly different, but not appreciably so.)

The vertical axis of the style box measures credit quality and is also broken into three groups: high, medium, and low. A fund's placement is determined by the average credit quality of all the bonds in its portfolio. Funds with high credit qualities tend to own either U.S. Treasury bonds or corporate bonds whose credit quality is just slightly below that of Treasuries. On the other hand, funds with low credit quality own a lot of high-yield, or junk, bonds. Medium-quality funds fall between the two extremes.

The style box can make it far easier for investors to find appropriate funds. Say you need a fund that carries only slightly more risk than a money market fund. Just look for funds that fall within the short-term, high-quality square of the style box. Or perhaps you want a rich income stream but aren't comfortable buying junk bonds. A fund that falls within the long-term, medium-quality square might be the answer. You can find the style box for all bond funds on their Morningstar Fund Reports.

Our Bond-Fund Buying Advice

Look for low costs.

A Wal-Mart mentality is a must when evaluating funds—even more so when the funds in question buy bonds. Because bonds typically gain less than stocks over time, their costs become a heavier burden. Costs are the most important factor when evaluating bond funds, hands down.

Note that, in addition to their expenses, high-cost bond funds often take on more risk than low-cost bond funds. Expenses get deducted from the income the fund pays to its shareholders, so managers of high-cost funds often do the darndest things to keep yields competitive, such as buying longer-duration or lower-quality bonds, or complex derivatives. In doing so, they increase the fund's risk.

Morningstar rates mutual funds, not individual bonds. When it comes to bond ratings, we reference the ratings that we receive from the mutual fund shops. And mutual fund shops tend to pull their ratings from one of three powerhouse bond-rating agencies: Standard & Poor's, Moody's, or Fitch Ratings.

A note about credit ratings— what Morningstar doesn't do

Managers with low expense hurdles, in contrast, can offer the same yields and returns without taking on extra risk. Plenty of terrific bond funds carry expense ratios of 0.75% or less.

Focus on total return, not yield.

Yield provides instant gratification in the form of regular income checks. But chasing yield can have its costs. Some funds use accounting tricks to prop up their yields at the expense of their principal, or net asset value (NAV). Managers will pay more than face value for high-yielding bonds and distribute that entire yield as the bonds depreciate to face value. Or they'll buy undervalued bonds and supplement their lower yields with capital gains. Both practices cut into NAV.

Investors sometimes accept dwindling NAVs for burly yields because they want the regular income that yields offer. Bad idea. Yield is nothing more than a percentage of NAV, so shrinking NAV leads to smaller income checks over time.

Imagine a $10,000 investment in a fund carrying an NAV of $10 and yielding 6.5%. One year later, the fund still yields 6.5%, but its NAV has slipped to $9. In that one year, income dropped from $650 to $585.

So instead of judging a bond fund by its yield, evaluate its total return—its yield plus or minus any capital appreciation or depreciation.

A note about credit ratings—what Morningstar does do	Morningstar does make distinctions between high and low credit quality.
	▸ High: Portfolio's average credit quality is AAA or AA.
	▸ Medium: Portfolio's average credit quality is lower than AA but greater than or equal to BBB.
	▸ Low: Portfolio's average credit quality is below BBB.

Seek some variety.

You wouldn't choose a fund that buys only health-care stocks as your first equity fund, so why should your first (and perhaps only) bond fund be a narrowly focused Ginnie Mae fund? Yet many investors own bond funds that buy only government bonds, or Treasuries, or mortgages.

For your first—and maybe only—bond fund, consider intermediate-term, broad-based, high-quality bond funds that hold both government and corporate bonds. Those investors in high tax brackets might consider municipal-bond funds, whose income is exempt from income taxes.

Fearless Facts

▶ Always buy low-cost funds. Bonds gain far less than stocks, so high costs can be really burdensome.

▶ Emphasize total return, rather than income, when judging your fund's prospects. Remember that a fund might boast an excellent yield, but that in the end, that yield could be drained from overall performance.

▶ Diversification is important in bond funds, too. You probably don't want an equity fund that focuses only on tech stocks, so why buy a bond fund that only shops in the health-care industry?

Quiz

1 Morningstar's fixed-income style box visually depicts a fund's:

   a Credit quality and duration.

   b Expenses and duration.

   c Total return and credit quality.

Answers to this quiz can be found on page 242

2 Bond funds with high expense ratios:

   a Usually return less than bond funds with low expense ratios.

   b Are riskier than bond funds with low expense ratios.

   c Both.

3 Which is likely the better bond fund over the long term?

   a Fund A with a 6% yield and a 5% total return.

   b Fund B with a 5% yield and a 6% total return.

   c Fund C with a 5% yield and a 5% total return.

4 According to Morningstar, which bond fund would be the best choice?

   a Fund A with an expense ratio of 1%, a duration of eight years, and an average credit quality of AAA.

   b Fund B with an expense ratio of 0.75, a duration of seven years, and an average credit quality of AA.

   c Fund C with an expense ratio of 0.5%, a duration of seven years, and an average credit quality of AA.

5 Which is least important when evaluating bond funds?

   a Their yields.

   b Their total returns.

   c Their expenses.

Worksheet

Take a look at one of your bond funds. Where does it lie in the Morningstar fixed-income style box? Based on the credit quality and interest-rate sensitivity of your fund, can you describe the type of environment in which it might do well? When might it tend to struggle?

Based on your fund's credit quality and interest-rate sensitivity, would you classify your bond fund's risks as high, medium, or low?

If you own more than one bond fund, are the funds investing in different parts of the bond market, or the same one? Would you say your bond funds offer adequate diversification across investment styles? If not, what style box should your next bond fund fall into?

Bond funds provide regular income through yield. But should yield be more important to an investor than total return? Why or why not?

continued...

How critical are expenses in selecting a bond fund for your portfolio? Why? Are any of your bond funds charging more than 0.75% in annual expenses? If so, do you think their costs are justified? Can you identify cheaper alternatives?

Lesson 216: Munis

Driving a Jaguar. Shopping at Neiman Marcus. Investing in municipal bonds.

These activities may seem exclusive to the rich and famous, but you don't need to be part of the elite to invest in municipal bonds. Investors in the highest tax bracket may profit most from municipal bonds' tax-exempt status, but investors in the lower tax brackets can benefit, too.

In this lesson, we'll find out how municipal bonds work, and why they are one of the last great tax breaks for investors. We'll then share Morningstar's hints for selecting a good municipal-bond fund.

What's a Muni?

States, cities, municipalities, and county governments can all issue municipal debt, or muni bonds, to raise money. They use the proceeds to improve roads, refurbish schools, or even build sports complexes. The bonds are usually rated by a major rating agency, such as Standard & Poor's or Moody's, based on the quality of the issuer.

Unlike income from bonds issued by corporations or the federal government, income generated by municipal bonds is exempt from federal and sometimes state income taxes. So when examining a municipal bond's yield, take the implicit tax advantage into account.

Let's take an example. Say you're an investor in the 25% tax bracket. You want to know which investment offers you a better yield: a corporate-bond fund yielding 7% or a muni-bond fund yielding 6%. After taxes, the muni fund is the higher yielding investment: Take 25% in taxes off the corporate-bond fund's 7% yield, and you're left with an aftertax yield of just more than 5%.

Muni-Fund Considerations

As you can see, municipal-bond funds can certainly be a compelling choice for the bond portion of your portfolio. If you decide that munis make sense for you, consider the following when searching for a suitable muni fund. (You can find much of this information on a Fund Report, in its shareholder report or prospectus, or on the fund family's Web site.)

Intermediate-Term Durations. As with most bond funds, a municipal-bond fund's value rises and falls depending on interest-rate changes. To determine a fund's interest-rate risk, check its duration. A long duration usually means greater potential for short-term gains and losses.

Vanguard Long-Term Tax Exempt's duration was roughly twice that of Thornburg Limited-Term Municipal National at the start of 1999. No wonder the Vanguard fund lost twice as much as the Thornburg fund (0.4% versus 0.2%) when interest rates rose in February of that year. But when rates fell in 2000, the Vanguard fund's longer-duration portfolio outpaced the Thornburg fund's, 13.3% to 6.8%.

Our suggestion: Choose the happy medium. In a jittery market, intermediate-term municipal-bond funds with durations between 4.5 and seven years have returned about 90% as much as long-term offerings, but with only about 70% of their volatility over the past five years.

Average Quality. Some municipal-bond funds are vulnerable to credit problems and bond defaults. (That is, the issuers of the bonds they own could fail to pay up on their obligations.) Some aren't.

Vanguard Insured Long-Term Tax Exempt, for example, only buys bonds that are insured against credit problems. Insured bonds earn AAA ratings (the highest) and are highly sensitive to interest-rate movements, but generally yield less than lower-quality bonds. On the other end of the credit spectrum lies Franklin High Yield Tax-Free Income, which invests heavily in lower-rated, higher-yielding munis.

For most of the 1990s, the strong economy masked the risks of high-yield municipal bonds. The average high-yield muni fund returned about 3% more annually than the average high-quality offering during the decade ending December 31, 1999. Roles reversed from 2000 through 2002, though, as the economy slowed and more municipalities threatened to default on their debts.

Here too, we recommend a middle-of-the-road approach: Favor funds with average credit qualities of AA. They have enough high-quality bonds to skirt most credit scares but are still flexible enough to snap up higher-yielding, lower-rated issues.

Know Your State's Tax Rate. Some municipal-bond funds invest all over the country, while others focus on a single state. National funds offer geographical diversification and can seize opportunities from New York to New Mexico.

Single-state funds, meanwhile, provide residents of some states with income that's exempt from both federal and state taxes. (National muni funds only give you the federal tax break.) A Californian doesn't pay the state income tax on the income from a California muni fund, and a resident of the Bay State avoids the Massachusetts tax on income from a Massachusetts fund.

Choose a single-state fund if you live in a high-tax state. Otherwise, go national for the diversification benefits.

| Identify your goals | The largest single-state muni categories belong to the coasts. Debt from New York and California, some of the country's most populated states, has always been popular with investors. In fact, muni bond funds that focus on these states are so numerous (and so different) that we distinguish between longer- and shorter-duration offerings. |

Seek Low Costs. Costs are important for all bond funds, but especially for municipal-bond funds. In any given year, the difference between the highest- and lowest-returning muni funds can be just a few percentage points. A small cost advantage therefore goes a long way. Invest in a muni fund with an expense ratio of less than 1%.

Avoid AMT, if Need Be. You can still owe taxes on the income of municipal-bond funds if you're exposed to the Alternative Minimum Tax (AMT) and the fund you own holds bonds subject to this tax. Fund managers buy bonds subject to the AMT because they tend to yield more than non-AMT bonds.

If you're concerned about the AMT, choose a muni fund that avoids bonds subject to the tax, such as T. Rowe Price Tax-Free Income. Fund family Web sites and prospectuses should spell out each fund's AMT policy.

Fearless Facts

▶ Remember that the main benefit of muni bond funds is their tax-exempt status. Do not bother to buy these funds for your tax-deferred retirement account!

▶ Focus on the golden mean. Rate and credit risk are often a problem with muni funds, too. After all, states and municipalities can default on their debt. Choose moderate funds with moderate durations and credit scores.

▶ Before you buy, make sure you can recite the following:
1. Your tax rate—otherwise, what's the point?
2. The cost structure of your fund.
3. Your fund manager's take on the Alternative Minimum Tax; you want to know exactly how much you'll be liable for down the road.

Quiz

1   Which is the higher-yielding bond fund after taxes for someone in the 28% tax bracket: a corporate bond fund yielding 7.5% or national municipal-bond fund yielding 6.0%?

a	The corporate bond fund.
b	The municipal-bond fund.
c	Their yields are the same after taxes.

Answers to this quiz can be found on page 243

2   Who issues municipal bonds?

a	Corporations.
b	The U.S. Treasury.
c	Municipalities, counties, or special projects.

3   Intermediate-term municipal bonds funds have:

a	Returned just as much as long-term muni-bond funds, with a lot more risk.
b	Returned far less than long-term muni-bond funds, with a lot less risk.
c	Returned nearly as much as long-term muni-bond funds, with less risk.

4   Assuming three municipal bonds mature at the same point in the future, which one likely yields the most?

a	The low-quality bond.
b	The high-quality bond.
c	The insured bond.

continued...

5   According to Morningstar, which is the best type of municipal-bond fund
     for most investors?

a	Fund A, a long-term fund with an average credit quality of AAA and an expense ratio of 1.15%.
b	Fund B, an intermediate-term fund with an average credit quality of B and an expense ratio of 1.0%.
c	Fund C, an intermediate-term fund with an average credit quality of AA and an expense ratio of 0.75%.

Worksheet

Who issues municipal bonds? What makes them an attractive investment? How do taxes play a role in the take-home return you earn from your bond fund?

What are five things to look for when investing in municipal-bond funds?

What would be the risk of buying an individual municipal bond rather than opting for a fund? Can you think of any potential benefits?
If you're a smaller investor, would you be better off in the bond or the bond fund?

continued...

What are the benefits of investing in single-state municipal-bond funds rather than national muni-bond funds? Investigate your state's tax treatment of municipal-bond income. Based on what you find out, would it be worth investing in a fund that focuses on bonds from your state or opting for a municipal-bond fund that owns bonds from several states?

If you're comparing the yields on municipal-bond funds with those of their taxable-bond rivals, you have to put the two competitors on equal footing. That means that you have to calculate the muni fund's tax-equivalent yield. The tax-equivalent yield tells you how much a taxable investment would have to yield in order to equal the aftertax return of the tax-exempt vehicle.

Try this with two funds, one a municipal-bond fund and the other a taxable fund. For a quick and dirty estimate of the muni fund's tax equivalent yield, take the yield of the tax-exempt fund and divide it by (one – your federal income-tax rate). Then compare that yield with that of the taxable fund.

Investing Terms

A

Alpha

A measure of the difference between a fund's actual returns and its expected performance, given its level of risk as measured by beta. A positive alpha figure indicates the fund has performed better than its beta would predict. In contrast, a negative alpha indicates the fund's underperformance, given the expectations established by the fund's beta. Alpha depends on two factors: the assumption that market risk, as measured by beta, is the only risk measure necessary, and the strength of the linear relationship between the fund and the index, as it has been measured by R-squared.

Annual Returns

Morningstar calculates annual total returns on a calendar-year and year-to-date basis. The year-to-date return is updated daily on Morningstar.com. For mutual funds, return includes both income (in the form of dividends or interest payments) and capital gains or losses (the increase or decrease in the value of a security). Morningstar calculates total return by taking the change in a fund's NAV, assuming the reinvestment of all income and capital-gains distributions (on the actual reinvestment date used by the fund) during the period, and then dividing by the initial NAV.

Unless total returns are marked as load adjusted, Morningstar does not adjust total return for sales charges or for redemption fees. Total returns do account for management, administrative, and 12b-1 fees and other costs automatically deducted from fund assets.

Automatic-Investment Plan

An arrangement by which investors may initiate an account with a fund with a very small investment up front, with the condition that they agree to invest a fixed amount per month in the future.

Average Credit Quality/Credit Quality

In Morningstar.com products, average credit quality gives a snapshot of the portfolio's overall credit quality. It is an average of each bond's credit rating, adjusted for its relative weighting in the portfolio. For corporate-bond and municipal-bond funds, Morningstar also shows the percentage of fixed-income securities that fall within each credit-quality rating, as assigned by Standard & Poor's or Moody's. U.S. government bonds carry the highest credit rating, while bonds issued by speculative or bankrupt companies usually carry the lowest credit ratings. Anything at or below BB is considered a high-yield or "junk" bond.

Average Weighted Price

Morningstar generates this figure from the fund's portfolio by weighting the price of each bond by its relative size in the portfolio. This number reveals if the fund favors bonds selling at prices above or below face value (premium or discount securities, respectively). A higher number indicates a bias toward premiums. This statistic is expressed as a percentage of par (face) value. Average weighted price can reflect current market expectations. Morningstar generates this figure from the fund's portfolio, by weighting the price of each bond by its relative size in the portfolio.

B

Bear Market

A period when investment values drop. Bear markets can exist for certain kinds of investments (such as small-company stocks), for an index (such as the S&P 500), or marketwide. Bear markets usually aren't labeled as such until values have slipped by 20%. Its opposite is called a bull market.

Bear Market % Rank

In Morningstar products, the bear-market percentile rank details how a fund has performed during bear markets. For stock funds, a bear market is defined as all months in the past five years that the S&P 500 lost more than 3%; for bond funds, it's all months in the past five years that the Lehman Brothers Aggregate Bond Index lost more than 1%. Morningstar adds a fund's performance during each bear-market month to arrive at a total bear-market return. Based on these returns, each fund is then assigned a percentile ranking. Stock funds are ranked separately from bond funds. Use this figure to analyze how well a fund performs during market downturns, relative to its peers.

Benchmark

What you compare your fund's returns with to judge its performance. A benchmark can be the average performance of funds similar to yours or a broad index of the investments your fund usually picks from. The S&P 500 Index is a good benchmark for funds that buy large-company stocks, for example.

Best Fit Alpha

In Morningstar products, this is the alpha of the fund relative to its Best Fit Index. Alpha is a measure of the difference between a fund's actual returns and its expected performance given its level of risk as measured by beta. A positive alpha figure indicates the fund has performed better than its beta would predict. In contrast, a negative alpha indicates the fund has underperformed given the expectations established by its beta.

Best Fit Beta

On Morningstar.com, this is the beta of the fund relative to its Best Fit Index. Beta is a measure of a fund's sensitivity to market movements. The beta of the market is 1.00 by definition. Morningstar calculates beta by comparing a fund's excess return over Treasury bills to the Best Fit Index's excess return over Treasury bills. A beta of 1.10 shows that the fund has performed 10% better than its Best Fit Index in up markets and 10% worse in down markets, assuming all other factors remained constant.

Best Fit Index

Morningstar defines this as the market index that shows the highest correlation with a fund over the most recent 36 months, as measured by the highest R-squared. Morningstar regresses a fund's monthly excess returns against the monthly excess returns of several well-known market indexes. Both the standard and best-fit results can be useful to investors. The standard index R-squared statistics can help investors plan the diversification of their portfolio of funds. For example, an investor who wishes to diversify and already owns a fund with a very high correlation (and thus high R-squared) with the S&P 500 might choose not to buy another fund that correlates closely to that index. In addition, the best-fit index can be used to compare the betas and alphas of similar funds that show the same best-fit index. Morningstar recalculates the best-fit index in-house on a monthly basis.

Beta

A measure of a fund's sensitivity to market movements. The beta of the market is 1.00 by definition. Morningstar calculates beta by comparing a fund's excess return over Treasury bills to the market's excess return over Treasury bills, so a beta of 1.10 shows that the fund has performed 10% better than its benchmark index in up markets and 10% worse in down markets, assuming all other factors remain constant. Conversely, a beta of 0.85 indicates that the fund is expected to perform 15% worse than the market during up markets and 15% better during down markets. Beta can be a useful tool when at least some of a fund's performance history can be explained by the market as a whole. Beta is particularly appropriate when used to measure the risk of a combined portfolio of mutual funds. It is important to note that a low beta for a fund does not necessarily imply that the fund has a low level of volatility. A low beta signifies only that the fund's market-related risk is low.

Bond

A loan you make to a company or government for a certain time (the bond's term or maturity) typically in return for regular interest payments (the bond's coupon). Interest from some government bonds, particularly municipal bonds, may be tax-free.

Broker

The "intermediary" between you and the other investors, a broker buys and sells securities for you for a fee, called a commission. There are many kinds of brokers, from online brokers, who allow you to trade cheaply over the Internet, to full-service brokers, who provide advice and other services.

Bull Market

A good time for investors! Stock prices rise during a bull market. And when stock prices go up, investors (usually) make money. Investors who think the stock market will continue to go up are called bulls. The opposite of a bull market is called a bear market.

C

Capital Appreciation

A gain in the value of a stock or bond. The amount of appreciation is measured by subtracting the purchase price from the current price.

Capital Gain/Loss

The difference between what you pay for a stock or other investment and what you sell it for. In other words, your profit or loss. If you buy shares of Great Company for $100 and sell them for $250, your capital gain is $150. You pay taxes on capital gains.

Cash Flow

Basically, what a company makes minus what it spends. A company's cash flow is its income (minus investment earnings) less what it spends on rent, equipment, and other costs. Some investors use cash flow instead of earnings to judge how well a company is doing.

Closed-End Funds

An investment that acts like a cross between a mutual fund and a stock. Like a mutual fund, it invests a pool of money in a variety of investments. Like a stock, however, it issues a limited number of shares that can trade at prices different from the value of its investments.

Closed Fund

An open-end fund that has closed, either temporarily or permanently, to new investors. This usually occurs when management finds the fund's increasing asset size to be disadvantageous.

Closed to All Investments

Funds that are accepting no investments whatsoever, even from current shareholders.

Closed to New Investments

If funds are closed to new investments, they are not accepting new shareholder investments. This does not, however, restrict current shareholders from increasing their investment amount.

Commission

What you pay a broker or financial advisor to buy or sell investments for you. Commissions can be a percentage of your trade (for example, 5% of a $10,000 trade equals a $500 commission) or a set fee. You usually pay a higher commission the more services your broker provides.

Composition

The composition percentages on Morningstar.com provide a simple breakdown of a fund's portfolio holdings, as of the date listed, into general investment classes. Cash encompasses both the actual cash and the cash equivalents (fixed-income securities with maturities of one year or less) held by the portfolio. Negative percentages of cash indicate that the portfolio is leveraged, meaning it has borrowed against its own assets to buy more securities or that it has used other techniques to gain additional exposure to the market.

Compounding

When your interest earns interest. If you invest $10,000 and generate a return of 10%, you'll have $11,000 at the end of the year. If you earn 10% again the next year, both your initial investment and your $1,000 in interest earn interest, for a new total of $12,100. Over time, compounding's effect is powerful.

Coupon

The fixed percentage paid out on a fixed-income security on an annual basis.

Credit Analysis

For corporate-bond and municipal-bond funds, the credit analysis depicts the quality of bonds in the fund's portfolio. The analysis reveals the percentage of fixed-income securities that fall within each credit-quality rating as assigned by Standard & Poor's or Moody's. At the top of the ratings are U.S. government bonds. Bonds issued and backed by the federal government are of extremely high quality and thus are considered superior to bonds rated AAA, which is the highest possible rating a corporate issue can receive. Morningstar gives U.S. government bonds a credit rating separate from AAA securities to allow for a more accurate credit analysis of a portfolio's holdings. Bonds with a BBB rating are the lowest bonds that are still considered to be of investment grade. Bonds that are rated BB or lower (often called junk bonds or high-yield bonds) are considered to be quite speculative. Like the style box, the credit analysis can help determine whether or not a fund's portfolio meets a desired standard or quality. It can also shed light on the management strategy of the fund. If the fund holds a large percentage of assets in lower-quality issues, for example, then the fund follows a more aggressive style and is probably more concerned with yield than credit quality.

Credit Risk

The chance that you won't be able to get interest payments or your money back from the issuer that sold you a bond. Government bonds have low credit risk, while junk bonds from companies with shaky credit have high credit risk.

D

Developed Markets

Morningstar characterizes the following as developed markets: Australia, Austria, Belgium, Canada, Denmark, Finland, France, Germany, Ireland, Italy, Japan, Luxembourg, the Netherlands, New Zealand, Norway, Singapore, Spain, Sweden, Switzerland, the United Kingdom, the United States, and a handful of smaller countries and territories (such as Gibraltar). All other countries are considered emerging markets. Emerging markets normally carry greater political and economic risk than developed countries, and stocks located in them are normally less liquid and more volatile.

Diversification

Spreading your money over many different investments. When you're diversified, if one investment does badly for a while, you may still make money from your other investments. Diversification generally lowers risk.

Dividends

Money taken from a company's profits and paid to stockholders. Companies aren't required to pay dividends. Dividends are paid to you either in cash or in more stock. Mutual funds that own dividend-paying stock must pass the dividends along to their shareholders each year.

Dollar-Cost Averaging

A way to buy more of an investment when it's cheaper and less when it's expensive. To dollar-cost average, you simply invest the same amount of money every week, month, or paycheck so that, as an investment's price falls, you automatically buy more shares.

Duration

One measure of the interest-rate sensitivity of a bond or bond fund. Bond funds with long durations will do well when interest rates are declining but suffer as interest rates rise. Short-duration bond funds are less volatile but offer fewer potential gains.

E

Earnings-per-Share Growth %

This figure for Morningstar products represents the annualized rate of net-income-per-share growth over the trailing one-year period for the stocks held by a fund. Earnings-per-share growth gives a good picture of the rate at which a company has grown its profitability per unit of equity. All things being equal, stocks with higher earnings-per-share growth rates are generally more desirable than those with slower earnings-per-share growth rates. One of the important differences between earnings-per-share growth rates and net-income growth rates is that the former reflects the dilution that occurs from new stock issuance, the exercise of employee stock options, warrants, convertible securities, and share repurchases.

Emerging Markets

Morningstar characterizes the following as developed markets: Australia, Austria, Belgium, Canada, Denmark, Finland, France, Germany, Ireland, Italy, Japan, Luxembourg, the Netherlands, New Zealand, Norway, Singapore, Spain, Sweden, Switzerland, the United Kingdom, the United States, and a handful of smaller countries and territories (such as Gibraltar). All other countries are considered emerging markets. Emerging markets normally carry greater political and economic risk than developed countries, and stocks located in them are normally less liquid and more volatile.

Enhanced-Index Funds

Like index funds, this group includes funds that attempt to match an index's performance. Unlike an index fund, however, enhanced-index funds typically attempt to better the index by adding value or reducing volatility through selective stock-picking.

Exchange-Traded Funds

At the most basic level, exchange-traded funds are just what their name implies: baskets of securities that are traded, like individual stocks, on an exchange. Unlike regular open-end mutual funds, ETFs are priced throughout the trading day. They can also be sold short and bought on margin—anything you might do with a stock, you can do with an ETF. They often also charge lower annual expenses than even the least costly index mutual funds. However, as with stocks, you must pay a commission to buy and sell ETF shares, which can be a significant drawback for those who trade frequently or invest regular sums of money.

Expense Ratio

The annual expense ratio, taken from the fund's annual report, expresses the percentage of assets deducted each fiscal year for fund expenses, including 12b-1 fees, management fees, administrative fees, operating costs, and all other asset-based costs incurred by the fund. Portfolio transaction fees, or brokerage costs, as well as initial or deferred sales charges are not included in the expense ratio. The expense ratio, which is deducted from the fund's average net assets, is accrued on a daily basis. Funds may also opt to waive all or a portion of the expenses that make up their overall expense ratio. The expense ratio is useful because it shows the actual amount that a fund takes out of its assets each year to cover its expenses. Investors should note not only the current expense-ratio figure, but also the trend in these expenses; it could prove useful to know whether a fund is becoming cheaper or more costly. Overall, expenses can have a meaningful impact on long-term results, so investors should try to invest in funds with below-average expenses.

F

Fees and Expenses

Morningstar distinguishes among the myriad fees and expenses encountered with mutual funds. The different expenses and their characteristics are listed as follows.

Administrative Costs—What your fund charges you in order to pay for its day-to-day operations, including renting office space, printing prospectuses, and keeping records. You'll never write a check for this fee, though, because administrative costs, like the other parts of your fund's expense ratio, are deducted directly from your fund's returns.

Deferred Load—Also called a contingent deferred sales charge or back-end load, a deferred load is an alternative to the traditional front-end sales charge, as it is deducted only at the time of sale of fund shares. The deferred-load structure commonly decreases to zero over a period of time. A typical deferred load's

structure might have a 5% charge if shares are redeemed within the first year of ownership and decline by a percentage point each year thereafter. These loads are normally applied to the lesser of original share price or current market value. It is important to note that although the deferred load declines each year, the accumulated annual distribution and services charges (the total 12b-1 fee) usually offset this decline.

Front-End Load—The initial sales charge or front-end load is a deduction made from each investment in the fund. The amount is generally based on the amount of the investment. Larger investments, both initial and cumulative, generally receive percentage discounts based on the dollar value invested. A typical front-end load might have a 4.75% charge for purchases less than $50,000, which decreases as the amount of the investment increases. Investors who have significant assets and work with a financial advisor are therefore better off buying front-load shares than deferred-load shares.

Management Fee—The management fee is the maximum percentage deducted from a fund's average net assets to pay an advisor or subadvisor. Often, as the fund's net assets grow, the percentage deducted for management fees decreases. Alternatively, the fund may compute the fee as a flat percentage of average net assets. A portion of the management fee may also be charged in the form of a group fee. To determine the group fee, the fund family creates a sliding scale for the family's total net assets and determines a percentage applied to each fund's asset base. The management fee might also be amended by or be primarily composed of a performance fee, which raises or lowers the management fee based on the fund's returns relative to an established index.

No-Load—These funds charge no sales or 12b-1 fees.

Redemption Fee—The redemption fee is an amount charged when money is withdrawn from the fund before a pre-determined period elapses. This fee usually does not go back into the pockets of the fund company, but rather into the fund itself and thus does not represent a net cost to shareholders. Also, unlike contingent-deferred sales charges, redemption fees typically operate only in short, specific time clauses, commonly 30, 180, or 365 days. However, some redemption fees exist for up to five years. Charges are not imposed after the stated time has passed. These fees are typically imposed to discourage market-timers, whose quick movements into and out of funds can be disruptive. The charge is normally imposed on the ending share value, appreciated or depreciated from the original value.

Service Fee—The service fee is part of the total 12b-1 fee. Capped at a maximum 0.25%, the service fee is designed to compensate financial planners or brokers for ongoing shareholder-liaison services, which may include responding to customer inquiries and providing information on investments. An integral component of level-load and deferred-load funds, the fees were previously known as a trail commission. Only service fees adopted pursuant to Rule 12b-1 are tracked. Despite the implication of its name, service fees do not act as compensation for transfer agency or custodial services.

12b-1—The 12b-1 fee represents the maximum annual charge deducted from fund assets to pay for distribution and marketing costs. This fee is expressed as a percentage. Some funds may be permitted to impose 12b-1 fees but are currently waiving all or a portion of the fees. Total allowable 12b-1 fees, excluding loads, are capped at 1% of average net assets annually. Of this, the distribution and marketing portion of the fee may account for up to 0.75%. The other portion of the overall 12b-1 fee, the service fee, is listed separately and may account for up to 0.25%. Often, funds charging a 12b-1 fee will allow shareholders to convert into a share class without the fee after a certain number of years. (These are normally deferred-load funds.)

Fixed Income

An investment that pays a specific interest rate, such as a bond, a certificate of deposit, or preferred stock. Mutual funds composed of fixed-income instruments (like bond funds) typically pay a variable rate of interest.

401(k) Plan

An employer-sponsored retirement plan. It lets you invest part of your paycheck—before taxes are deducted—in investments, such as mutual funds, that you choose from the plan. Your 401(k) money isn't taxed until you start withdrawing it, usually at retirement.

Fund Advisor

This is the company or companies that are given primary responsibility for managing a fund's portfolio.

Fund Family

A fund family is a company that offers mutual funds. Generally speaking, the company name is included in the official fund name.

Fund Inception Date

The date on which the fund began its operations. Funds with long track records offer more history by which investors can assess overall fund performance. However, another important factor to consider is the fund manager and his or her tenure with the fund. Often a change in fund performance can indicate a change in management.

Fund of Funds

A mutual fund that invests in other mutual funds. The goal is to give you maximum diversification with a single investment. You might think of it as buying an assortment of chocolates in a box, rather than separately. One difference: With a fund of funds, you often pay extra for the "box."

G

Growth Measures

Book-Value Growth—Book value is, in theory, what would be left over for shareholders if a company shut down its operations, paid off all its creditors, collected from all its debtors, and liquidated itself. In practice, however, the value of assets and liabilities can change substantially from when they are first recorded. Book-value growth shows the rate of increase in a company's book value per share, based on up to four periodic time periods. When reported for a mutual fund, it shows the weighted average of the growth rates in book value for each stock in the fund's portfolio. This measure helps determine Morningstar's growth score for each stock and the overall growth orientation of the fund.

Cash-Flow Growth—Cash flow tells you how much cash a business is actually generating from its earnings before depreciation, amortization, and noncash charges. Sometimes called cash earnings, it's considered a gauge of liquidity and solvency. Cash-flow growth shows the rate of increase in a company's cash flow per share, based on up to four time periods. When reported for a mutual fund, it shows the weighted average of the growth in cash flow for each stock in the fund's portfolio. This measure helps determine Morningstar's growth score for each stock and the overall growth orientation of the fund.

Growth of $10,000 Graph—The Growth of $10,000 graph shows a fund's performance based on how $10,000 invested in a fund would have grown over time. The returns used in the graph are not load-adjusted. The growth of $10,000 begins at the date of the fund's inception, or the first year listed on the graph, whichever is appropriate.

Historical Earnings Growth—Historical earnings growth shows the rate of increase in a company's earnings per share, based on up to four periodic time periods. When reported for a mutual fund, it shows the weighted average of the growth in earnings for each stock in the fund's portfolio. This measure helps determine Morningstar's growth score for each stock and the overall growth orientation of the fund.

Long-Term Earnings Growth—Earnings are what is left of a firm's revenues after it pays all of its expenses, costs, and taxes. Companies whose earnings grow faster than those of their industry peers usually see better price performance for their stocks. Projected earnings growth is an estimate of a company's expected long-term growth in earnings, derived from all polled analysts' estimates. When reported for a mutual fund, it shows the weighted average of the projected growth in earnings for each stock in the fund's portfolio. This measure helps determine Morningstar's growth score for each stock and the overall growth orientation of the fund.

Sales Growth—Sales growth shows the rate of increase in a company's sales per share, based on up to four periodic time periods, and is considered the best gauge of how rapidly a company's core business is growing. When reported for a mutual fund, it shows the weighted average of the sales-growth rates for each stock in the fund's portfolio. This measure helps determine Morningstar's growth score for each stock and the overall growth orientation of the fund.

H

Hedge Fund

A hedge fund is like a mutual fund on steroids. Most hedge funds have really high minimum investments, often $1 million or more, and are allowed to make risky investments that mutual funds aren't. Hence, they can make and lose lots of money.

I

Index Funds

Funds that track a particular index and attempt to match its returns. While an index typically has a much larger portfolio than a mutual fund, the fund's management may study the index's movements to develop a representative sampling and match sectors proportionately.

Individual Retirement Account (IRA)

A tax-deferred retirement account that permits individuals to set aside tax-deferred earnings each year. IRAs can be established at a bank, mutual fund, or brokerage.

Institutional Funds

A mutual fund that generally only sells shares to big players such as pension plans. The typical institutional fund has a high minimum investment, typically $100,000 or more. You may be able to get into an institutional fund for less through online brokers or an employer retirement plan.

Interest-Rate Sensitivity

How much the value of a bond or bond fund changes when interest rates shift. Bond values move in the opposite direction from interest rates. Duration is one common measure of interest-rate sensitivity.

L

Lifecycle Funds

These funds are designed to be an investor's sole investment. Usually designated as aggressive, moderate, or conservative, these funds typically hold a mix of stocks and bonds.

Liquidity

A way to describe how easily you can sell an investment for cash. Your savings account, for instance, has lots of liquidity, because you can get at your money any time. Stocks that are traded a lot are also very liquid. Little-known stocks and most collectibles are considered illiquid.

M

Management Team

This applies to funds in which there are two or more people involved in fund management, and they manage together, or when the fund strongly promotes its team-managed aspect.

Manager Tenure

This represents the number of years that the current manager has been the portfolio manager of the fund. Fund management is clearly an important variable in fund performance. If you buy a fund for its long-term performance, for example, you'll want to be sure that the manager responsible for the good record is still at his or her post. Likewise, if an improvement in fund performance correlates with the arrival of a new manager, investors should downplay the fund's previous record and focus on the performance attributable to the new management.

Market Capitalization

For domestic-stock offerings, this measures the portfolio's "center of gravity," in terms of the size of companies in which it invests. A market capitalization is calculated for each stock. Its weight in the average weighted market-cap calculation is then determined by the percentage of stocks it consumes in the overall portfolio. For example, a stock that is a 10% position in a fund will have twice as much influence on the calculation than a stock that is a 5% stake.

Market-Neutral Funds

These are funds that attempt to eliminate the risks of the market, typically by holding 50% of assets in long positions in stocks and 50% of assets in short positions. Funds in this group match the characteristics of their long and short portfolios, keeping factors such as P/E ratios and industry exposure similar. Stock-picking, rather than broad market moves, should drive a market-neutral fund's performance.

Market Risk

The chance that an entire group of investments, such as U.S. stocks, will lose value (as opposed to one particular stock falling in price). Market risk is a danger because there's always the chance you'll have to sell an investment when the market is down.

Market-Timing

This is an investment strategy in which investors switch in and out of securities or between types of mutual funds in the hopes of benefiting from various economic and technical indicators that are thought to presage market moves.

Market Value

The current value of the security. For stocks, the market value is the security price times the number of shares held.

For bonds, the market value is the bond price multiplied by the number of bonds held.

Maturity

How long you must wait before a bond repays you. For instance, a 30-year bond pays you interest for 30 years, then repays you your investment, or principal. The longer the maturity, the riskier the bond, because you must wait longer before reinvesting your money.

Mean

Represents the annualized total return for a fund over 3-, 5-, and 10-year time periods.

Minimum Investments

Initial Investment—The minimum purchase indicates the smallest investment amount a fund will accept to establish a new account.

Additional Investment—This indicates the smallest additional purchase amount a fund will accept in an existing account.

Initial Auto-Invest Program

Investment—This indicates the smallest amount with which one may enter a fund's automatic-investment plan—an arrangement in which the fund takes money on a monthly, quarterly, semi-annual, or annual basis from the shareholder's checking account. The systematic investment amount is the minimum amount required for subsequent regular investments in an automatic investment plan. Studies indicate that regular automatic investment, also known as dollar-cost averaging, is perhaps the most successful investment plan for long-term investors.

Additional Auto-Invest Program

Investment—This indicates the smallest additional investment amount a fund will accept in an existing automatic-investment plan account.

Money Market—Similar to a savings account, only usually paying you a better interest rate. Money-market funds invest in extremely short-term instruments. As a result, they're ultrasafe and you can withdraw exactly what you've deposited at any time.

Morningstar Category

While the investment objective stated in a fund's prospectus may or may not reflect how the fund actually invests, a Morningstar category is assigned based on the underlying securities in each portfolio. Morningstar categories help investors and investment professionals make meaningful comparisons between funds. The categories make it easier to build well-diversified portfolios, assess potential risk, and identify top-performing funds. We place funds in a given category based on their portfolio statistics and compositions over the past three years. If the fund is new and has no portfolio history, we estimate where it will fall before giving it a more permanent category assignment. When necessary, we may change a category assignment based on recent changes to the portfolio.

Domestic-Stock Funds—Funds with at least 70% of assets in domestic stocks are categorized based on the style and size of the stocks they typically own. The style and size divisions reflect those used in the Morningstar style box: value, blend, or growth style and small, medium, or large median market capitalization.

International-Stock Funds—Stock funds that have invested 40% or more of their equity holdings in foreign stocks (on average over the past three years) are placed in one of the following international-stock categories:

Europe—At least 75% of stocks invested in Europe.

Japan—At least 75% of stocks invested in Japan.

Latin America—At least 75% of stocks invested in Latin America.

Diversified Pacific—At least 65% of stocks invested in Pacific countries, with at least an additional 10% of stocks invested in Japan.

Asia/Pacific ex-Japan—At least 75% of stocks invested in Pacific countries, with less than 10% of stocks invested in Japan.

Diversified Emerging Markets—At least 50% of stocks invested in emerging markets.

Foreign—An international fund having no more than 20% of stocks invested in the United States.

World—An international fund having more than 20% of stocks invested in the United States.

World Allocation—Used for funds with stock holdings of greater than 20% but less than 70% of the portfolio where 40% of the stocks and bonds are foreign.

Bond Funds—Funds with 80% or more of their assets invested in bonds are classified as bond funds. Bond funds are divided into two main groups: taxable bond and municipal bond. (Note: For all bond funds, maturity figures are used only when duration figures are unavailable.)

Taxable-Bond Funds

Long-Term Government—A fund with at least 90% of bond portfolio invested in government issues with a duration of greater than or equal to 6 years, or an average effective maturity of greater than 10 years.

Intermediate-Term Government—A fund with at least 90% of its bond portfolio invested in government issues with a duration of greater than or equal to 3.5 years and less than 6 years, or an average effective maturity of greater than or equal to 4 years and less than 10 years.

Short-Term Government—A fund with at least 90% of its bond portfolio invested in government issues with a duration of greater than or equal to one year and less than 3.5 years, or average effective maturity of greater than or equal to one year and less than four years.

Long-Term Bond—A fund that focuses on corporate and other investment-grade issues with an average duration of more than 6 years, or an average effective maturity of more than 10 years.

Intermediate-Term Bond—A fund that focuses on corporate, government, foreign, or other issues with an average duration of greater than or equal to 3.5 years but less than or equal to 6 years, or an average effective maturity of more than 4 years but less than 10 years.

Short-Term Bond—A fund that focuses on corporate and other investment-grade issues with an average duration of more than one year but less than 3.5 years, or an average effective maturity of more than one year but less than four years.

Ultrashort Bond—Used for funds with an average duration or an average effective maturity of less than one year. This category includes general- and government-bond funds, and excludes any international, convertible, multisector, and high-yield bond funds.

Bank Loan—A fund that invests primarily in floating-rate bank loans instead of bonds. In exchange for their credit risk, these funds offer high interest payments that typically float above a common short-term benchmark.

Emerging-Markets Bond—A fund that invests at least 65% of assets in emerging-markets bonds.

High-Yield Bond—A fund with at least 65% of assets in bonds rated below BBB.

Multisector Bond—Used for funds that seek income by diversifying their assets among several fixed-income sectors, usually U.S. government obligations, foreign bonds, and high-yield domestic debt securities.

World Bond—A fund that invests at least 40% of bonds in foreign markets.

Municipal-Bond Funds

Municipal National Long-Term—A national fund with an average duration of more than 7 years, or average maturity of more than 12 years.

Municipal National Intermediate-Term—A national fund with an average duration of more than 4.5 years but less than 7 years, or average maturity of more than 5 years but less than 12 years.

Municipal National Short—A fund that focuses on municipal bonds with an average duration of less than 4.5 years, or an average maturity of less than 5 years.

High-Yield Municipal—A fund that invests at least 50% of assets in high-income municipal securities that are not rated or that are rated by a major rating agency at the level of BBB (considered speculative in the municipal industry) or below.

State-Specific Munis—A municipal-bond fund that primarily invests in one specific state. These funds must have at least 80% of assets invested in municipal bonds from that state. Each state-specific muni category includes long, intermediate, and short-duration bond funds.

Morningstar Rating for Funds

A measure of how well a mutual fund has balanced risk and return. We compare a fund's long-term risk-adjusted performance with that of its category peers. A 5-star rating is the best; 1 star is the worst.

Morningstar Risk

An assessment of the variations in a fund's monthly returns, with an emphasis on downside variations, in comparison to similar funds. In each Morningstar Category, the 10% of funds with the lowest measured risk are described as Low Risk, the next 22.5% Below Average, the middle 35% Average, the next 22.5% Above Average, and the top 10% High. Morningstar Risk is measured for up to three time periods (3, 5, and 10 years). These separate measures are then weighted and averaged to produce an overall measure for the fund. Funds with less than three years of performance history are not rated.

Multiple Managers

This refers to the arrangement in which two or more people are involved in the fund management, and they manage independently; quite often the fund has divided net assets in set amounts among the individual managers. In most cases, multiple managers are employed at different subadvisors or investment firms.

Mutual Fund

An investment company that sells shares to people and uses the money to buy stocks, bonds, and other investments. The mutual fund passes on the earnings from its investments to its shareholders. Mutual funds are an easy way for individuals to invest in a lot of securities at once.

N

NAV

A fund's net asset value (NAV) represents its per-share price. A fund's NAV is derived by dividing the total net assets of the fund, less fees and expenses, by the number of shares outstanding.

Net Income Growth %

This figure for Morningstar products represents the annualized rate of net-income growth over the trailing one-year period for the stocks held by a fund. Net-income growth gives a good picture of the rate at which companies have grown their profits. All things being equal, stocks with higher net-income growth rates are generally more desirable than those with slower net-income growth rates. Morningstar aggregates net-income growth figures for mutual funds using a median methodology, whereby domestic stocks are ordered from highest to lowest based on their net-income growth rates. One adds up the asset weighting of each holding until the total is equal to or greater than half of the total weighting of all domestic stocks in the fund. The net-income growth rate for that stock is then used to represent the net-income growth rate of the total portfolio.

P

Portfolio

All the investments you own or, similarly, all the investments your fund owns.

Potential Capital-Gains Exposure

The percentage of a fund's total assets that represent capital appreciation. In other words, this is how much of the fund's assets would be subject to taxation if the fund were to liquidate today. Where a negative number appears, the fund has reported losses on its books. This information (realized and unrealized appreciation and net assets) is taken from the fund's annual report. Although funds rarely liquidate their entire portfolio, a fund with a higher potential capital gains exposure may be more likely to realize large capital gains in the event of a manager change or strategy shift. A high capital-gains exposure often accompanies a low turnover strategy, wherein a fund holds stocks over the long term, allowing profits to accumulate.

Price/Book Ratio

The price/book (P/B) ratio of a fund is the weighted average of the price/book ratios of all the stocks in a fund's portfolio. Book value is the total assets of a company, less total liabilities (sometimes referred to as carrying value). A company's price/book value is calculated by dividing the market price of its outstanding stock by the company's book value, and then adjusting for the number of shares outstanding. (Stocks with negative book values are excluded from this calculation.)

Price/Cash-Flow Ratio

This represents the weighted average of the price/cash-flow ratios of the stocks in a fund's portfolio. Price/cash-flow represents the amount an investor is willing to pay for a dollar generated from a particular company's operations. Price/cash-flow shows the ability of a business to generate cash and acts as a gauge of liquidity and solvency. Because accounting conventions differ among nations, reported earnings (and P/E ratios) may not be comparable across national boundaries. Price/cash-flow attempts to provide an internationally standard measure of a firm's stock price relative to its financial performance.

Price/Earnings Ratio

The price/earnings (P/E) ratio of a fund is the weighted average of the price/earnings ratios of the stocks in a fund's portfolio. The P/E ratio of a company, which is a comparison of the cost of the company's stock and its trailing 12-month earnings per share, is calculated by dividing a stock's price by its earnings. In computing the average, Morningstar weights each portfolio holding by the percentage of equity assets it represents, so that larger positions have proportionally greater influence on the fund's final P/E. A high P/E usually indicates that the market will pay more to obtain the company's earnings because it believes in the firm's ability to increase its earnings. (P/Es can also be artificially inflated if a company has very weak trailing earnings, and thus a very small number in this equation's denominator.) A low P/E indicates the market has less confidence that the company's earnings will increase; however, a fund manager or an individual with a 'value investing' approach may believe such stocks have an overlooked or undervalued potential for appreciation.

Price/Sales Ratio

This represents the weighted average of the price/sales ratios of the stocks in a fund's portfolio. Price/sales represents the amount an investor is willing to pay for a dollar generated from a particular company's operations.

Prime-Rate Funds

These funds invest in senior corporate loans and senior secured debt securities. These funds anticipate paying dividends that float or reset at a margin above a generally recognized rate such as LIBOR (London Inter-Bank Offer Rate).

Principal

The money you originally invested. It can also mean the face value of a bond, which you get back when the bond matures. You don't count income or capital gains as principal for an investment, even if you reinvest them.

Projected Earnings Growth %

This figure on Morningstar.com represents the projected one-year earnings growth rate of the stocks held by a fund. Projected earnings growth gives a good picture of a company's growth projects. All things being equal, stocks with better growth prospects are more desirable than those with poorer growth rates. Morningstar aggregates projected earnings growth figures for mutual funds using a median methodology, whereby domestic stocks are ordered from highest to lowest based on their projected earnings growth. One adds up the asset weighting of each holding until the total is equal to or greater than half of the total weighting of all domestic stocks in the fund. The projected earnings growth rate for that stock is then used to represent the projected one-year earnings growth rate of the total portfolio.

Prospectus

A guide legally required by the SEC that explains many of the details about a mutual fund. Always read the prospectus before making an investment. A mutual fund's prospectus will tell you how the fund picks investments, how much it has made in the past, and what its major risks are.

Qualified Access

This is any fund offered through a retirement plan such as an employee pension plan, 401(k), or 403(b) plan. These plans meet the necessary IRS requirements to allow participants to deduct the amount of their investments from their taxable income, thereby investing pretax dollars. Money builds up on a tax-deferred basis, and when the investor withdraws money, both the principal and profit are treated as taxable income.

R

Return

The amount of money your investment made for you. Usually return is given as a percentage of the amount you invested, so a $5,000 investment that made you $400 earned an 8% return ($400 divided by $5,000).

Revenue Growth

This figure represents the rate of revenue growth over the trailing one-year period for the stocks held by a fund. Revenue growth gives a good picture of the rate at which companies have been able to expand their businesses. All things being equal, stocks with higher revenue growth rates are generally more desirable than those with slower revenue growth rates.

Role in Portfolio

Morningstar designates funds as core, supporting player, or specialty. Core funds should be the bulk of an investor's portfolio, while supporting players contribute to a portfolio but are secondary to the core. Specialty offerings tend to be speculative and should typically only be a small portion of investors' portfolios.

R-Squared

The percentage of an investment's returns explained by movements in a benchmark index. An S&P 500 index fund will have an R-squared of nearly 100 compared with the S&P 500 Index, since they move in step, but would have a much lower one compared with a gold index.

S

Sector Fund

A mutual fund that invests in companies in a specific type of business. Sector funds can invest in a general industry, such as technology companies, or a specific industry, such as Internet companies. Because they focus on only one industry, they're usually riskier than general stock funds.

Sector Risk

The danger that the stock of many of the companies in one sector (such as health care or technology) will fall in price at the same time because of an event that affects the entire industry.

Shareholder Report

A guide your mutual fund sends out at least twice per year with information on how the fund is doing and what investments it owns. It usually includes a letter from your fund's president and/or manager.

Sharpe Ratio

This risk-adjusted measure was developed by Nobel Laureate William Sharpe. It is calculated by using standard deviation and excess return to determine reward per unit of risk. The higher the Sharpe ratio, the better the fund's historical risk-adjusted performance. The Sharpe ratio is calculated for the past 36-month period by dividing a fund's annualized excess returns over the risk-free rate by its annualized standard deviation. It is recalculated on a monthly basis. Since this ratio uses standard deviation as its risk measure, it is most appropriately applied when analyzing a fund that is an investor's sole holding. The Sharpe ratio can be used to compare directly how much risk two funds each had to bear to earn excess return over the risk-free rate.

Socially Responsible Funds

These funds, also known as SRI funds, invest according to noneconomic guidelines. Funds may make investments based on such issues as environmental responsibility, human rights, or religious views. For example, socially responsible funds may take a proactive stance by selectively investing in environmentally friendly companies or firms with good employee relations. This group also includes funds that avoid investing in companies involved in promoting alcohol, tobacco, or gambling, or those in the defense industry.

Standard Deviation

This statistical measurement of dispersion about an average depicts how widely a mutual fund's returns varied over a certain period of time. Investors use the standard deviation of historical performance to try to predict the range of returns that are most likely for a given fund. When a fund has a high standard deviation, the predicted range of performance is wide, implying greater volatility. Standard deviation is most appropriate for measuring the risk of a fund that is an investor's only holding. The figure cannot be combined for more than one fund because the standard deviation for a portfolio of multiple funds is a function of not only the individual standard deviations, but also of the degree of correlation among the funds' returns.

Subadvisor

In some cases, a mutual fund's advisor employs another company, called the subadvisor, to handle the fund's day-to-day management. In these instances, the portfolio manager generally works for the fund's subadvisor, and not the advisor.

Target-Retirement Funds

These funds are managed for investors planning to retire—or to begin withdrawing substantial portions of their investments—in a particular year. The funds follow an asset-allocation strategy that grows more conservative as the target date nears.

Taxable Account

An investment account that isn't sheltered from taxes. This means you have to pay taxes on any interest payments or distributions, as well as on any gains you realize when you sell the investment. With tax-deferred accounts, such as IRAs and 401(k)s, you can postpone the payment of these taxes.

Tax-Adjusted Return

These returns are adjusted for taxes and sales charges and follow the SEC guidelines for calculating returns before sale of shares. The tax-adjusted return shows a fund's annualized after-tax total return for the 5- and 10-year periods, excluding any capital-gains effects that would result from selling the fund at the end of the period. To determine this figure, all income and short-term capital-gains distributions are taxed at the maximum federal rate at the time of distribution. Long-term capital gains are taxed at a 20% rate. The after-tax portion is then reinvested in the fund. State and local taxes are ignored, and only the capital-gains are adjusted for tax-exempt funds, as the income from these funds is non-taxable.

Tax-Cost Ratio

This represents the percentage-point reduction in an annualized return that results from income taxes. The calculation assumes investors pay the maximum federal rate on capital gains and ordinary income. For example, if a fund made short-term capital-gains and income distributions that averaged 10% of its NAV over the past three years, an investor in the 35% tax bracket would have a tax-cost ratio of 3.5 percentage points. The 35% tax rate was used for illustrative purposes. However, our tax-cost calculation uses the maximum income-tax rate that applied during the year in which the distribution was made.

Tax-Deferred

An account that lets you wait before paying taxes on your earnings. Your defined contribution account is tax deferred since you only pay taxes on earnings when you withdraw them, not when you earn them. Because more of your money works for you through compounding, tax deferral allows you to earn more.

Tax-Exempt

Off-limits to the Internal Revenue Service. Few investments are completely tax-exempt. Interest from city bonds, for example, is usually free from federal taxes but may be subject to state taxes. Earnings on Roth IRA investments are tax-exempt because you never pay taxes on them.

Tax-Managed Funds

These funds are managed with a sensitivity to tax ramifications. They try to minimize taxable distributions through various methods.

Total Cost Projections

Found in a fund's prospectus, these figures show how much an investor would expect to pay in expenses—sales charges (loads) and fees—over the next 3, 5, and 10 years, assuming a $10,000 investment that grows by 5% per year with redemption at the end of each time period. Total cost projections are commonly based on the past year's incurred fees or an estimate of the current fiscal year's fees, should a portion of the overall fee structure change as of the printing of the fund's most current prospectus. Newer funds are required to print total cost projections for 1- and 3-year time periods only since longer-term projections may not be possible to estimate.

Total Return

A fund's gain, in percentage terms, over a specified period of time. Total return consists of any income the fund paid out, plus (or minus) any increase (or decrease) in the value of the portfolio's holdings. We assume reinvestment of income and capital-gains distributions in our calculations. Returns are not adjusted for sales charges or redemption fees.

Trailing 12-Month Yield

Yield is the percentage income your portfolio returned over the past 12 months. It is calculated by taking the weighted average of the yields of the stocks and funds that compose the portfolio. Dividend yield for the underlying stocks and funds is calculated by dividing the total dollar amount the security paid out as income to shareholders by the share price. Note that for mutual funds, the dollar-income value includes interest income from fixed-income securities, dividends from stocks, and realized gains from currency transactions.

Turnover Ratio

This is a measure of the fund's trading activity, which is computed by taking the lesser of purchases or sales (excluding all securities with maturities of less than one year) and dividing by average monthly net assets. A turnover ratio of 100% or more does not necessarily suggest that all securities in the portfolio have been traded. In practical terms, the resulting percentage loosely represents the percentage of the portfolio's holdings that have changed over the past year. A low turnover figure (20% to 30%) would indicate a buy-and-hold strategy. High turnover (more than 100%) would indicate an investment strategy involving considerable buying and selling of securities. Morningstar does not calculate turnover ratios. The figure is culled directly from the financial highlights of the fund's annual report.

V

Volatility

Refers to fluctuations in the performance of an investment. A money-market account with a fixed $1 share price has no volatility, but a mutual fund that invests in stocks might be very volatile. In general, investments that generate large returns are more volatile than investments with lower returns.

Y

Yield

The interest or dividends your investments produce. It doesn't include capital gains, which you may receive when you sell an investment. Yield is figured as a percentage of the investment's worth. A $100 bond yielding 5% pays you $5 a year.

Recommended Readings

Common Sense on Mutual Funds: New Imperatives for the Intelligent Investor by John C. Bogle, 2000. Published by John Wiley & Sons. The best book on funds, period.

Classics: An Investor's Anthology by Charles D. Ellis with James R. Vertin, 1990. Published by Business One Irwin.

Asset Allocation: Balancing Financial Risk by Roger C. Gibson, 2000. Published by McGraw-Hill Trade. An essential text that has influenced a whole generation of financial advisors.

The Intelligent Investor: The Definitive Book on Value Investing, Revised Edition by Benjamin Graham, Jason Zweig, 2003. Published by Harper Business. The wisdom in this book still resonates decades after its publication.

Security Analysis: The Classic 1934 Edition by Benjamin Graham and David L. Dodd, 1996. Published by McGraw-Hill Trade. This book is considered by many top managers to be the bible of investing.

Buffett: The Making of an American Capitalist by Roger Lowenstein, 1996. Published by Main Street Books. A great biography. You cannot call yourself a serious investor and not be a student of Buffett.

One Up on Wall Street: How to Use What You Already Know to Make Money in the Market by Peter Lynch, 2000. Published by Simon & Schuster. This classic is one of the most accessible books on picking individual stocks.

A Random Walk Down Wall Street by Burton G. Malkiel, 2004. Published by WW Norton & Company. Makes the case for indexing and shows how much of what we attribute as brilliance among managers may really be random chance.

The Wall Street Journal Guide to Understanding Money and Investing by Kenneth M. Morris, Virginia B. Morris, and Alan M. Siegel, 2004. Published by Fireside. This user-friendly guide provides novices with solid money and market information.

continued...

The New Commonsense Guide to Mutual Funds by Mary Rowland, 1998. Published by Bloomberg Press. Rowland's guide is the perfect choice if you would rather not spend a lot of time reading about funds—or want to read about them in short, digestible chunks.

The Money Game by Adam Smith, 1976. Published by Vintage. While the attitudes are dated, this remains a great history.

The Only Investment Guide You'll Ever Need by Andrew Tobias, 2002. Published by Harvest Books. A great introduction to thinking about the key trade-offs of personal finance.

The Money Masters and the New Money Masters by John Train, 1994. Published by HarperBusiness. Wonderful introductions to some of the best money managers ever.

Additional Morningstar Resources

In addition to this workbook, Morningstar publishes a number of products about mutual funds. There's something for everyone, from newsletters to sourcebooks. Most can be found at your local library, or by calling Morningstar to start your own subscriptions (866-608-9570).

Morningstar® Mutual Funds™

This twice-monthly report service features full-page financial reports and analysis of 1,600 funds specially selected for building and maintaining balanced portfolios. Our report service is favored by professionals and serious investors and carried in more than 4,000 libraries nationwide. Trial subscriptions are available.

Morningstar® FundInvestor™

Monthly newsletter offers 48 pages of fund investing help—including Morningstar model portfolios, analysis of funds, funds to avoid, the FundInvestor 500, and Morningstar Analyst Picks.

Morningstar.com

Our Web site features investing information on funds, stocks, bonds, retirement planning, and more. In addition to powerful portfolio tools, you'll find daily articles by Morningstar analysts and editors. Much information on the site is free, and there's a reasonably priced Premium Membership service for investors requiring more in-depth information and sophisticated analytical tools.

Morningstar® Funds 500™

Annual book of full-page reports on 500 selected funds. The new edition appears in January of each year and includes complete year-end results of funds covered, as well as general fund industry performance information.

Morningstar Guide to Mutual Funds
5-Star Strategies for Success

Here's the perfect desktop resource for new and experienced investors. Encapsulating 20 years of experience analyzing funds, it shows you what works in fund investing. In addition to plain-English chapters on key topics, it includes real-world examples and 14 investor checklists. Hardbound, 6″x 9″, 286 pages.

Answer Key

Quiz 201: Benchmarks

1   c.   It's tempting to pick a fund that returns more than you need, but remember: The greater the return, the greater the potential for loss. Be sure the fund you pick has a history of returning as much as your benchmark, or you may not meet your goal.

2   b.   The DJIA is too narrow a benchmark for most large-company funds, and the MSCI EAFE Index follows international stocks.

3   b.   The S&P 500 includes mostly large-company stocks, and the Lehman Brothers Index follows bonds. Neither is an appropriate benchmark for small-company funds.

4   b.   In this case, the S&P 500 is probably a bad benchmark for this fund. It likely owns something other than large-company stocks and could very well look great relative to its Morningstar category peers.

5   b.   Though the S&P 500 is a fine benchmark for all types of large-company funds, the Morningstar category is better when analyzing large-cap growth or other specific types of funds. The DJIA is too narrow a benchmark for most large-company funds.

Quiz 202: Looking at Historical Risk, Part One

1   b.   Standard deviation is not a relative measure; beta is. Moreover, a fund can theoretically have a low standard deviation and still lose money while a fund with a high standard deviation can never lose a dime.

2   b.   Future returns will fall within one standard deviation (returns between 2% and 22% in this case) of a fund's average return 68% of the time and within two standard deviations (returns between -8% and 32%) 95% of the time.

233

3 c. Standard deviation is not a relative measure. To determine whether a fund's standard deviation is high or low, compare it with the standard deviations of other funds or of an index.

4 c. A fund with a beta of 1.20 is 20% more volatile than the index. So if the index falls, the fund will fall 1.20 times as much—here, 12%.

5 a. The lower the R-squared, the less reliable beta is as a measure of volatility; the closer to 100 the R-squared is, the more reliable the beta. Standard deviation and R-squared have nothing to do with each other.

Quiz 203: Looking at Historical Risk, Part Two

1 b. Morningstar compares the risk of each fund with other funds in the same Morningstar category.

2 c. Both Morningstar measures treat U.S. equity funds and bond funds separately, so you can't use them to compare a stock fund with a bond fund. Standard deviation is an absolute figure, so you can use it to compare the two funds.

3 b. If you seek funds that offer a narrow range of returns, examine standard deviation. If you want funds that rarely underperform, look for low Morningstar Risk scores.

4 b. Morningstar Risk is based on the idea that investors are more concerned about a probable loss than an unexpectedly high gain.

5 c. Morningstar Risk describes the variation in a fund's month-to-month returns, with an emphasis on downward variation.

Quiz 204: Gauging Risk and Return Together, Part One

1　b.　Alpha hinges on beta, not standard deviation. Funds with positive alphas have returned more than their betas suggested they would return.

2　c.　With its beta, you'd expect Fund C to gain 8% (10% x 0.8 = 8%). It made almost twice that. Fund A should have gained 10%, so it earns a lower alpha than Fund C. Fund B should have returned 17%, so the fund has a negative alpha.

3　c.　Alphas aren't meaningful unless the fund's R-squared is greater than 75. Sharpe ratios, meanwhile, are always useful because they involve standard deviations rather than betas.

4　a.　To calculate Sharpe ratio, subtract the T-bill return from the fund's return, and divide by standard deviation.

5　c.　The Sharpe ratio is based on the relationship between a fund's risk as measured by standard deviation and its returns.

Quiz 205: Gauging Risk and Return Together, Part Two

1　c.　Star ratings are not subjective, nor are they meant to predict short-term winners. Star ratings are created mathematically, and they are based on historical risk and return.

2　c.　Morningstar rates funds, not managers; as a result, star ratings don't change when managers leave funds.

3　a.　Very low returning funds are unlikely to earn high ratings, as are modest-risk, modest-return funds.

4 c. The Morningstar Rating identifies funds that have historically performed well on a risk-adjusted basis, relative to their peers.

5 a. Morningstar rates all funds for up to three periods—the trailing 3, 5, and 10 years.

Quiz 206: Examining a Stock Fund's Portfolio, Part One

1 c. The style box provides a snapshot of the size and price of the stocks in a fund's portfolio. To get a feel for how rapidly a fund manager buys and sells stocks, check a fund's turnover rate.

2 a. A company's market capitalization is simply its size based on the market value of its shares. It has nothing to do with earnings or sales.

3 c. Larger companies are often more established and tend to be more predictable than smaller companies; therefore, their stock prices tend to be steadier.

4 b. Both price/book and price/earnings ratios tell you how expensive a stock is based on some value—either the value of the company if it were sold and paid off its debts (P/B) or the value of a company based on its earnings (P/E).

5 c. Funds that own expensive (growth) small companies are bound to be more volatile than those that own large, inexpensive (value) stocks or middle-of-the-road (blend) fare are.

Quiz 207: Examining a Stock Fund's Portfolio, Part Two

1   b.   If a fund has 50% of its portfolio in the technology sector, for example, half of its performance will be determined by the strength or weakness of that one sector.

2   b.   The greater a fund's price/earnings multiple, the greater its price risk.

3   c.   Funds with fewer holdings are more vulnerable to troubles in one or two stocks than funds with more holdings are. Sector weightings reveal a fund's sector risk, while P/E and P/B ratios relative to a fund's peers reflect price risk.

4   c.   Buy-and-hold managers will have lower turnover rates than managers who buy and sell stocks on short-term factors.

5   c.   The last fund is taking on more price risk (its P/E is higher than the other funds' P/E) and per-issue risk than the others (its number of holdings is smaller), and it is trading more aggressively.

Quiz 208: Why Diversify?

1   c.   You often get better short-term results as you are likely to own something that is doing well. Diversification lowers long-term volatility as different investments move in and out of favor. But diversification doesn't mean you'll never lose money.

2   a.   Very short-term investments, such as money market funds, are the only ways to truly safeguard against losses. Sometimes even the best-diversified portfolio loses money.

3   c.   Diversifying by investment and asset class are most important. Diversifying by subasset class is secondary.

4   b.   Owning multiple companies is diversification by investment, while owning a mix of growth, value, and international stocks is generally seen as diversification by subasset class.

5   c.   There are no "must-own" types of funds; assembling a portfolio of mutual funds is a matter of personal taste and personal goals. However, be aware of your options so that you can appropriately choose what you should and shouldn't own.

Quiz 209: Building Your Mutual Fund Portfolio

1   c.   Investing is about compromise. You can't have everything. Low risk and high returns rarely go together.

2   a.   Your core funds should be your portfolio anchors, the funds you rely on to reach your goals. For many, large-cap funds fill the bill. Emerging-markets and tech funds are too risky to be at the core of most investors' portfolios.

3   c.   Core funds shouldn't be exciting. They are reliable stock funds and bond funds. Excitement and variety should come from your noncore holdings.

4   a.   You don't need noncore funds, and if you are investing in a tax-deferred account, taxes don't matter to you.

5   c.   It depends on the funds. If the 10-fund portfolio owns all large-cap growth funds and the 2-fund portfolio contains a broad-based index fund and a bond fund, the latter would be more diverse. More funds don't necessarily mean more diversification.

Quiz 210: Choosing an Index Fund

1 **b.** It's hard to choose among the hundreds of index funds, and not all index funds are tax-friendly. But a good index fund is a low-maintenance investment; asset growth and manager changes don't matter, and it won't change its investment style.

2 **c.** Not all index funds are cheap—not even all large-blend index funds are. Index funds in the large-blend category can follow different indexes—the most common of which is the S&P 500.

3 **a.** Small-cap index funds reap big taxable gains when companies grow too large for the index, forcing the fund to sell those stocks. Large-cap and S&P 500 index funds sell stocks when they fall out of the index, meaning they only sell small positions.

4 **c.** Given that index-fund managers aren't actively researching and selecting stocks, all index funds ought to be cheap. Too bad not all of them are.

5 **b.** The Russell 2000 is the most commonly used index for tracking small-company stocks.

Quiz 211: SRI Funds

1 **c.** Although most SRI funds shun tobacco, alcohol, and nuclear-weapons manufacturers, they can screen on dozens of different criteria. There's no single approach.

2 **b.** Although generally considered to be unfriendly to the environment, an oil company could be held in an environmentally concerned SRI fund if that fund takes a relative approach. That's why it's important to understand how a fund's screens work.

3   a.   Some SRI funds engage in shareholder activism to reform companies. Others simply shun those companies.

4   c.   These funds are often smaller than non-SRI funds and therefore don't enjoy the same economies of scale. Further, some SRI funds charge higher management fees, taking into account the added costs of SRI screening and research.

5   a.   Building an all-SRI portfolio can be difficult. There just is not an abundance of good choices in some areas of the market, especially bonds and international stocks.

Quiz 212: Choosing an International Fund, Part One

1   c.   Many international funds do well when U.S. funds aren't doing quite as well. As a result, they offer both good return potential and diversification.

2   c.   While you should certainly examine a fund's Morningstar rating and its past returns, you must also understand how the fund invests— the sort of companies it owns and the countries they're from.

3   a.   Emerging-markets stocks behave unlike U.S. stocks and thus make great diversifiers. They also can post exhilarating returns. But they're exceptionally high risk.

4   b.   Funds with substantial emerging-markets positions may not be categorized as emerging-markets funds. Check the fund's exposure to Latin America and the Pacific Rim to get a sense of how much it invests in emerging markets.

5   c.   A Latin America fund is both a regional and emerging-markets fund at the same time, and it would therefore be the most volatile of the group.

Quiz 213: Choosing an International Fund, Part Two

1 c. During some time periods, international small-cap funds may outperform international large-cap funds; during other periods, they'll underperform. But they always tend to be more volatile.

2 a. Although most international funds used to invest mostly in moderately priced large companies, today's international funds can invest in growth or value stocks from large or small companies.

3 c. You get the stock's return along with the change in value of the local currency versus the U.S. dollar.

4 b. While you've lost money on the stock, you made a profit on the pound's rise against the dollar.

5 a. Because you've hedged your currency exposure, it doesn't matter what the pound does; your returns are affected only by the stock's performance—and in this case, that means you've lost money.

Quiz 214: Bond Funds, Part One

1 b. When interest rates rise, bond prices fall. Bond prices and interest rates have an inverse relationship.

2 a. Duration measures a bond's interest-rate sensitivity. Credit quality is itself a measure of the creditworthiness of the company that issued the bond. Yield is based on the income the bond pays to its owners.

3 c. Duration is the indicator of interest-rate risk. The longer the duration, the more sensitive a fund is to interest-rate changes.

4 a. Credit quality is the indicator of credit risk. A fund with an average credit quality of B is taking on more credit risk than one with investment-grade quality such as A or AAA.

5 c. Lower-rated high-yield bonds will do poorly during a recession, as issuers will have a tougher time meeting their high debt payments.

Quiz 215: Bond Funds, Part Two

1 a. While examining total return and expenses is important, our style boxes show the characteristics of the securities that funds own—in this case, duration and credit quality.

2 c. To overcome high expenses, bond fund managers generally take on more risk to keep their yields and returns competitive.

3 b. Fund A is losing its principal (its yield is greater than its total return). Fund C is treading water. Fund B is generating more total return than yield and is thereby increasing its income payouts over time. Always focus on total return, not just yield.

4 c. First of all, this fund is the lowest cost of the group, and cost is the most important factor when evaluating bond funds. Next, its duration is lower than fund A's, so it's not taking on as much interest-rate risk as Fund A is.

5 a. Yield is nothing more than a percentage of principal, so it's more important to examine a fund's total return than its yield. Further, expenses are perhaps the most important factor to consider when investing in bond funds.

Quiz 216: Munis

1 b. The aftertax yield on the corporate bond fund is just 5.4% (or 7.5% x 0.72) while the aftertax yield on the municipal-bond fund is its stated yield of 6.0%.

2 c. Corporations issue corporate bonds while the U.S. Treasury issues Treasuries.

3 c. With their shorter durations, intermediate-term funds are less sensitive to interest-rate movements and are therefore less volatile. Yet intermediate-term funds have been competitive when it comes to their returns.

4 a. Insured bonds are the highest-quality possible in the municipal-bond landscape, and high-quality bonds generally yield much less than lower-quality bonds. Lower-quality bonds yield more because of their credit risk.

5 c. For most, Fund C, a low-cost, intermediate-term fund of reasonably high credit quality is the best choice.

Also in the Morningstar Fearless Investing Series

Find the Right Mutual Funds

Our beginning-level workbook shows you how to find mutual funds best meeting your investing objectives.

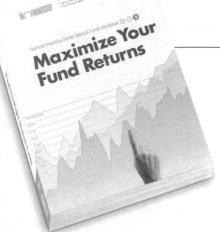

Maximize Your Fund Returns

In this advance-level workbook, you'll learn how to rebalance your portfolio, calculate your personal rate of return, and more.

Coming in Summer 2005—Morningstar Fearless Investing Series for Stocks